P9-DEP-358

post-Rapture
Radio

post-rapture radio

lost writings from a failed revolution

russell rathbun

JOSSEY-BASS
A Wiley Imprint
www.josseybass.com

Copyright © 2005 by Russell Rathbun. All rights reserved.

Published by Jossey-Bass
A Wiley Imprint
989 Market Street, San Francisco, CA 94103-1741   www.josseybass.com

No part of this publication may be reproduced, stored in a retrieval system, or transmitted in any form or by any means, electronic, mechanical, photocopying, recording, scanning, or otherwise, except as permitted under Section 107 or 108 of the 1976 United States Copyright Act, without either the prior written permission of the Publisher, or authorization through payment of the appropriate per-copy fee to the Copyright Clearance Center, Inc., 222 Rosewood Drive, Danvers, MA 01923, 978-750-8400, fax 978-646-8600, or on the web at www.copyright.com. Requests to the Publisher for permission should be addressed to the Permissions Department, John Wiley & Sons, Inc., 111 River Street, Hoboken, NJ 07030, 201-748-6011, fax 201-748-6008, e-mail: permcoordinator@wiley.com.

Jossey-Bass books and products are available through most bookstores. To contact Jossey-Bass directly call our Customer Care Department within the U.S. at 800-956-7739, outside the U.S. at 317-572-3986, or fax 317-572-4002.

Jossey-Bass also publishes its books in a variety of electronic formats. Some content that appears in print may not be available in electronic books.

All scripture references are taken from the New Revised Standard Version of the Bible unless otherwise noted or misquoted through my own sloppiness.

Unless otherwise noted, scripture is taken from the New Revised Standard Version Bible, copyright 1989, Division of Christian Education of the National Council of the Churches of Christ in the United States of America. Used by permission. All rights reserved.

Library of Congress Cataloging-in-Publication Data
Rathbun, Russell.
Post-rapture radio: lost writings from a failed revolution / Russell Rathbun.
  p. cm.
 ISBN 0-7879-7393-9 (alk. paper)
 1. Christianity—21st century. 2. Christianity and culture. I. Title.
BR121.3.R38   2005
277.3'083—dc22   2004026725
Printed in the United States of America

FIRST EDITION
HB Printing   10 9 8 7 6 5 4 3 2 1

contents

FOR my DAD,
who taught me how to preach

prelude to the apocalypse

The box came from a friend, Clark Morphew, who was, until recently, the religion writer for the St. Paul daily newspaper.

When he was clearing out his cubicle in preparation for his retirement, he invited me in to look through the hundreds of books that publishers had sent him over the years to review, to see if there was anything I wanted. I was kneeling on the ground, going through stacks of New Age self-help books and apocalyptic novels, when I saw the box.

It was the handwriting on the address label that attracted me. It had an urgent, maybe demented quality to it. There was no return address, just my friend's name, the name of the paper, and the ZIP code for downtown St. Paul. It was incomplete—no postage. It must have been hand-delivered.

The box had been opened, so I folded back the flaps. Sitting on top of a pile of manuscripts and scraps of paper inside was a note in the same urgent hand:

Having exhausted my own resources, I commend these writings to you. Perhaps you may find a way to use them.

Yours in the mercy of Christ,
Rev. Richard Lamblove

The box contained what looked like hundreds of sermons, random notes, and other writings. Tucked in against the side of the box was a journal. I wasn't completely sure what I had here, but just looking through some of the pages, *unknown-crazy-preacher* seemed a real possibility, and that is just about my favorite nonfiction genre. Not that I had *read* in this genre before, but I had heard it a lot. I make a habit of listening to unknown-crazy-preachers on the radio in my car. I have developed such a fine-tuned ear for these fellows that when I am scanning the stations, I can tell right away if I have found something. There is the awkward pause between syllables: "Ezek . . . iel," "Pow . . . er," "Jes . . . us," followed by a rush of words: "came-into-this-world-to-save-every-man-woman-and-child-from-the-eternal-ungodly-tortures-of-the-pit-of-hell." This comes out sounding like somebody struggling to push a baby carriage up one side of a steep hill and then letting it go at the top. Then there's the hiss and hum of poor recording equipment and the inevitable address of the listeners as friends: "Friends, let me tell you the end is coming, not someday but soon."

And the *gnosis*—that secret knowledge that is missed by the common believer. "Now I know you think you're saved. You think things with you and Jesus are just fine, but unless you are in accord with Revelation 5:15 and know the power it unlocks in Daniel 14, well, friend you're in for a big surprise. It's not e . . . nough to . . . know the pow . . . er of Je . . . sus. You-have-to-know-how-to-claim-it-hold-it-tight-and-use-it-amen."

This box gave me that same feeling—that I had encountered a genuine, unvarnished American character.

I do not know what intrigues me about these preachers. It is like Outsider Art or Folk Literature. Perhaps it is a kind of cultural slumming. The way those guys plead and yell and threaten, making huge logical leaps, with no time to slow down and show their math. Their rhetorical style belongs to another age. It is refreshingly offensive and infuriating. Compared to the soft and amusing "relevant life application messages" given by their Evangelical brothers and sisters, or the egghead theses delivered in a kindly drone by their more distant relations in the American mainline

Protestant mausoleum churches, it is actually compelling—crazy, illogical, folk theology at its worst. But compelling.

I *listen* to these sermons. Which is something I can rarely do. I have an affliction common to many churchgoers: the 20-Minute Coma. When the preacher stands up and his mouth starts moving, all my brain activity (except that necessary to maintain vital functions) ceases. Try as I might (and I might, but more likely, I might not), I cannot make myself pay attention. But with these crazy radio preachers, I pay attention. This could of course be attributed to the fact that I am driving a car at the time and that my life depends on staying alert.

If only some of that element could be introduced into a Sunday-morning-at-church sermon. If my life depended on staying alert and listening, I could be cured of the 20-Minute Coma. But I know nothing as threatening or life-changing as a car accident will happen at church.

But really, it is more than the need not to crash that keeps the coma away while listening to these preachers. Maybe it's the passion, the certainty of belief. They know the truth and cannot resist the compulsion to proclaim it to the world—to preach it. Nothing seems to impede them, not the lack of education, or of natural ability, or of any assurance that a single soul is listening. I have never been that convinced about anything in my life, certainly not God's word for the masses. But these unknown-crazy-preachers at least present, for me, the possibility of that kind of belief.

I asked Clark about the box. He only remembered that it had arrived sometime in the last couple of years and was thrown in a corner along with the many other unsolicited rantings and self-published revelations he had received from readers and, for one reason or another, had yet to recycle.

I spent the next hour and a half going through the box, reading the journal, randomly selecting sermons and the odd notes. The notes were all recorded with a thin-tipped black magic marker on the insides of decimated cereal boxes, other processed-food packaging, and pages apparently cut or torn from books that had nothing to do with the subjects addressed. It was as if he had run out of paper and was so consumed with a thought that he grabbed the closest thing at hand to write on.

One of these random writings—a critique of Ben Greg, a popular mega-church pastor and church consultant, starts on the pages of *How to Win Friends and Influence People,* continues on the title page of *Understanding Mental Illness,* and concludes on the inside of a Trix cereal box.

Among the notes was what appears to be a verse-by-verse commentary on the book of Revelation. It is written on pages torn from *Left Behind: A Novel of the Earth's Last Days,* as if he were trying to rewrite the book. But—and this confused me at first—the handwriting in those notes was different from that on the box. I could tell it was the same person writing because of the strange blocky capitals and oddly slanted "tall" letters. But some of the notes seemed carefully composed, scholarly in a way. They didn't appear to be hurriedly written. The pages were not in order, though. They were scattered throughout the box, and much of the work (if there ever was a complete work) was missing.

The more I read, the more a picture of this preacher emerged. He was certainly an unknown-crazy-preacher, but he was not an extreme theological or political conservative. Believe me, this is rare in the unknown-crazy-preacher genre. And he was no low-brow, old-school, yelling-and-threatening, logic-leaping firebrand, although he did share some of the same qualities. Although he was clearly somewhat educated, he displayed, at times, sloppy thinking and confusing rhetoric. But he had that passion for proclaiming a truth that he clearly believed could change the world. He believed that proclamation—preaching—mattered.

And he was a *revolutionary*—a self-proclaimed revolutionary—apparently in the service of a self-proclaimed revolution.

The journal, obviously handmade, was bound with the cover from a church growth "how-to" book titled, *The New Church for the New Century: Growing Awesome Congregations Through Real, Relevant, and Relational Worship.* It looked like he had gone over it with sandpaper. Then in red he had stenciled, "The Manifesto for the Beginning of the Old Revolution."

From the journal entries it seems clear the Rev. Lamblove had been, at one time, an Evangelical who became "born again"✷ and was now convinced that Evangelicals, in a race to appear increasingly relevant (and as a means of saving the souls of America), had gone too far. Instead of merely imitating contemporary culture, they came to help define it, "trading ecclesiology for business management practices, Evangelism for marketing, and the sermon for self-help motivational speeches."✷

Because of his conversion and in the face of what he saw as the ever-growing dominance of a Contemporary Christian Culture Conspiracy (Lamblove's term), he proclaimed a revolution that would bring down this Babylon, using the sermon as his only weapon. He writes in an undated journal entry:

The sermon is the weapon of choice for this revolution—it is dangerous, inexpensive, and readily available. While long abandoned by the Contemporary Christian Culture Conspiracy as irrelevant

---

✷ I use this term cautiously but decidedly. In the history of the American church, the term ceased to be two words taken from the third chapter of the gospel according to St. John and became a signifier. Whether applied to oneself or to another, it is shorthand for identifying who is *in,* that is, which one of us clearly knows and holds "right doctrine." My use of the term here is to indicate the opposite. It is clear that Rev. Lamblove has spent most of his life "inside" but has had a transformational experience that has moved him outside the camp of American Evangelicalism. Perhaps I should say "born again—again."

✷ From a journal entry that starts on the inside cover of Lamblove's journal titled, "Revolution: Why and How."

old technology, when set properly in a service of worship it becomes like rocks, bricks, a Molotov cocktail. ❋

This is certainly high regard for the sermon. And a bit nuts—but compelling. What if it were true?

It is certainly what St. Luke would have us believe. Recounting Jesus' seminal sermon at Nazareth, the gospel writer tells how our savior took for his text a passage from Isaiah and brought it home with a proclamation that a revolution had begun. So powerful was this sermon that when he finished, "all in the synagogue were filled with wrath. And they rose up and put him out of the city, and led him to the brow of the hill on which the city was built, that they might throw him down headlong."

And what about Stephen? He preaches one of the great sermons in the history of the church. He goes on for a whole chapter. So powerfully does he brandish this weapon of the sermon that the hearers respond by stoning him to death.

What if sermons could be that powerful—could proclaim a revolution, incite mobs, be something more important than a preventer of car crashes? What if Lamblove were right? What if a sermon didn't have to be the same Sunday school lesson so many of us have heard for the last thirty-five years (and the Sunday school lesson wasn't even that good to begin with)? What if it could be like a rock, or a brick, or a Molotov cocktail thrown into the hollow center of culture to ignite passion, depth, meaning?

Of course, these instances with Jesus and Stephen are examples of the congregation throwing things back. And in the end, they did both end up being killed. (This is what I mean about Lamblove's sloppy thinking.) But maybe that would have been a more satisfying end for the good Reverend. It seems that the response to his revolution was indifference. At least that is what his

---

❋ Ibid.

note from the box indicates, and I have heard no accounts of a congregation killing its pastor after the sermon in recent years.

I am not sure if Rev. Lamblove's critique is primarily cultural or theological; both elements are certainly present. I am not sure that Lamblove knows himself. To give him more credit, he might claim that the two are inseparable, although my impression is that he has not thought it out. His writing seems to be more instinctual than well reasoned.

The cultural critique

If the critique is primarily cultural, then the Rev. Lamblove has picked the wrong target. His revolution is too narrow. Why affix the Christian label to his foe? It is really Contemporary Culture *in toto* he finds fault with. Contemporary Culture *is* shallow and overly individualistic and consumed with the kind of status measured by money and power and celebrity. And American Evangelicalism can be seen to have similar failings. But that is because it is peopled with, well, people, who happen to be alive at a certain place and time and whose religious practices are integrated with the rest of their lives. *Of course* a successful religious movement reflects popular culture! American Evangelicalism *has* been integrated with the culture as a whole. That is a sign of its success. American Evangelicalism, along with Fundamentalist Islam, seems to be one of the few recent success stories of a religious movement in the world.

The time in which Lamblove is writing is precisely when the movement we now know as American Evangelicalism took form and came to be the important cultural and religious presence it is today. The movement can be credited, without exaggeration, with preserving Christianity's place in American culture. The liberalism that gained dominance in mainline Protestantism as a response to fundamentalism's anti-rational, separatist stance left the church full of thinking, caring individuals. But the church was missing the theological center that compelled commitment. Furthermore, the intellectualism left the average American churchgoer with a god (rarely identified as Jesus, just God) they could neither understand nor recognize—a reserved and distant creator without passion, suggesting vague principles about the goodness of humanity.

The history of the second half of the twentieth century shows that people go to church primarily because they believe in Jesus. When that belief is replaced with a social agenda or is merely a cultural expectation, the attendance numbers begin to drop. The empty churches of Europe had long proved this reality by the time the Evangelicals began their ascent.

Mainline Protestant denominations have experienced an alarming, uninterrupted decline in attendance since the early 1960s. That same period of time saw small groups of disaffected and primarily young believers forming independent worship communities that did away with the antiquated, rigid structures of their parents' church and found a worship language and music that spoke to them. They recast Jesus as their friend—a highly personal, feeling friend, who was not constricted in the way their parents' Jesus was. Nor was he above sitting crossed-legged on the ground.

Early examples of "praise songs" from this period are obviously influenced by the folk rock of the times. This is no different from what successful church movements have always done. The venerated hymn "Be Thou My Vision" is an Irish folk melody from the 1700s. John Wesley freely admitted putting new words to English pub songs to create relevant worship songs.

As these young believers grew up, their churches and their Jesus grew up with them. And while, like their parents, they got jobs and careers, had families, bought houses, and consumed, they insisted on doing all of these things in a *new* way.

Their "new way" churches reflected not the structures of the old (and now unquestionably dying) institutional denominations but the structures that were recognizable and welcoming to their peers.

This new noninstitutional church organization's architecture borrowed from movie theaters and shopping malls—places that were recognizable and comfortable. These new church buildings were not only more appropriate for the worship styles of this budding movement but served their evangelistic purposes as well.

A seeker would never consider entering an antique building, dark and dour, to listen to old-fashioned music and hear an oddly costumed professor give a speech. But it was not a stretch for that same seeker to pull into the new church's large parking lot, enter the wide glass doors, sit in the theater-style seats, watch a band play familiar-sounding music, and hear a person dressed in regular clothes share a little bit about life.

For Lamblove to find fault with the American Evangelical church (what he calls Contemporary Christian Culture)—a movement that has done so much to revitalize a stagnating faith—because it had "moved so rapidly toward cultural relevance that it overshot its mark, not merely addressing the popular culture in a language it could comprehend but so thoroughly aping its veneer that it became indistinguishable from its target, in some cases influencing it to the point of replacing it," as he says, is to find fault with its success.

What else would a successful church movement be than one that speaks the relevant truths of Christianity in a relevant way? Did not the original church "planter" do the same thing? Is a parable anything more than the PowerPoint presentation of its day?

Would Lamblove choose a faith that stood *outside* the culture it inhabited?

One wonders if Lamblove is the sort that has always been an outsider in culture and his chosen profession. His inability to fit in is a likely motivation for his vitriol against American Evangelicalism. Is the Rev. Richard Lamblove mad at popular culture *because* it is popular? Is he mad at popular Christian culture *because* he could find no comfort in it? Escalating the despair and anger one would expect of a perpetual outsider to the point of declaring a revolution, remaking the American Evangelical church into a Contemporary Christian Culture Conspiracy suggests some sort of imbalance.

But you can't have unknown-crazy-preacher without the crazy. And here I have an unknown-crazy-*revolutionary*-preacher.

тнe тнeological critique

If the Rev. Lamblove's critique is primarily theological, then I'll have to beg off. Though I am an ordained Christian minister, I am a failed one. And while my early journey does mirror his, I was never "born again" as he means it. I was born again once when I was a preadolescent, but I was never "born again—again" in the Lamblovian sense. Where he found fault in the culture of faith he inherited and sought to rectify the situation, I found fault and gave up—sort of.

I took a leave of absence from my congregation and have been working part-time at a coffee shop. The rest of my time was supposed to be dedicated to figuring things out but was more occupied with red wine and Japanese cartoons, that is, until I found the box and the Rev. Richard Lamblove. I originally suspected that Clark had invited me to come and look through his books in the hopes that one of them might spark something in me—"rekindle my faith," as they say. His invitation did result in giving me something more constructive to do than drink and watch television. But as far as any "rekindling"—I'm sorry Clark, but the project has confirmed my belief in the church as simply a necessary and benign cultural institution, which in my estimation does not diminish it; religious institutions are a valuable part of every culture and, when vital, can serve as its core.

It is for this reason that I have limited my comments on Lamblove's sermons and writings to one of a biographer. Although it is clear that he thought essential theological issues were at stake in the American Evangelicalism embrace of contemporary culture,

I am most interested in the story of an individual. Therefore, my primary focus in assembling these writings will be an attempt to tell the story of the Rev. Richard Lamblove.

However, I am telling a story that I don't actually know. The task of presenting Lamblove's various journal-entry rants and cereal box notes, together with his sermons and musings on the book of Revelation, has not been an easy task. I have tried to assemble them chronologically, but there are no dates on anything—not the notes, not the sermons, and not even the journal entries.

Based on the biblical texts he used for his sermons, I have surmised that the entire period covered by his journal is only about nine months of his life in either 1998 or 2000. I cross-checked his chosen Bible verses with the lectionary✢ to establish this timeline. Because the chronology is so questionable, and I need at least some way, however tenuous, to organize this material, I have chosen as a broad outline to mirror the book of Revelation. This seemed appropriate, given his ongoing commentary on the book in his notes. Besides, it is the only thing among all his writings that has a discernable sequence. If one wants to tell a story, there has to be a minimal suggestion of a sequence of events.✢ Also please note that I have included my comments on the text in two ways:

✢ The lectionary is a calendar of scripture verses prescribed for each Sunday of the year. It is used by the Catholic church and most mainline Protestant denominations. However, assuming Lamblove followed the lectionary is not necessarily a reliable assumption, given that most Evangelical churches do not follow it. My assumption is based on his mention of it in one of his notes, and there does seem to be some correspondence between his choices and those in the lectionary.

✢ Mirroring Revelation also seems an appropriate organizational structure, given that it is generally seen as a sequence of events leading to the end of the world but is actually a series of seven cycles in which the same things keep happening over and over again and at the same time. So it really is not a sequence of events at all but multiple attempts at explaining *the* event. It is nonnarrative taken for narrative, which is a good description of what I have done with Lamblove's writings.

"Editor's Comments" at the beginning of each section and "Notes" scattered throughout. The Editor's Comments allow me to provide contextual information, and the Notes allow commentary with a minimum of interruption.

Second, and to a much lesser degree, I focus on his misguided critique of the American Evangelical culture because it is an integral part of his passion for proclamation. And it's bizarre, which makes it interesting to me. I have consciously left out any comment on his theological critiques or assertions. In my leave of absence, I have taken a vow of theological abstinence. *Absence* and *abstinence*. It is ironic that these terms, which could have easily described the faith of my youth, now describe the nonfaith of my adulthood.

Alora, beyond the contents of this box, there is no record of any such revolutionary movement at the end of the last century. And I can find no record of a Rev. Richard Lamblove. Even before I convinced Clark to use all his expertise as a journalist and the resources of his newspaper to track the Reverend down, he said, "The name is obviously made up. It sounds made up." And it does.

Whoever he is or was, he has left this record of his failed revolution, which fell into my hands and which I now commend to you, dear friends.

Rev. Russell Rathbun
Editor

The writings contained in this thin volume
are the work of one man. The failed revolution
they served appears to be the same.

post-rapture radio

post-Rapture Radio
part one

the Apocalypse

Editor's Comment

. . . .

What I am calling Lamblove's "commentary on the book
of Revelation" was written on pages torn from
LEFT BEHIND, by Tim La Haye and Jerry Jenkins.
He's describing a sort of lexicon.

From Lamblove's commentary on the Book of Revelation

Terms Related to the End of the World

Revelation

The word *revelation* is the English translation of the Greek word *apokalypsis* or "apocalypse," which means, in effect, pulling back a veil in order to reveal something. Jacques Derrida notes that the first use of this term in the Greek translation of the Bible appears in the ninth chapter of Genesis. Noah had built the ark and survived the hardship of the flood; he had found dry land, and God had blessed him and made a covenant with him, so he sort of thought he could relax. He did what people do to relax after surviving such adversity. "He planted a vineyard; and he drank of the wine, and became drunk, and lay uncovered in his tent" (Gen. 9:20b–21). Noah's son Ham pulled back the veil of the tent and revealed his father's nakedness: the first apocalypse in the Bible. The final apocalypse in the Bible is basically the same thing, except this time it is the church caught with its pants down.

Eschatology

Eschatology is the systematic theological category that concerns itself with the end of time. It has been used to explain the end of the world, where every horror is an allegorical imperative, perpetuating the fear of God's judgment, elucidating the suffering that will come to the evildoers, and ensuring the end of this God-forsaken world.

But eschatology as it is actually practiced is *scatology.* It is read as a book that is concerned with the scat of popular culture. Instead of pointing to Jesus Christ as the definitive revelation, it points us to our own feces, where we can examine what has been digested. We can determine what we have been taking in. We can understand the diet of fear, manipulation, and complacency we have been feasting on.

I think this may be a helpful way of reading the book of Revelation.

Editor's Comment
....

The following selection is from his notes. It was
written on the front and back of an envelope
bearing the SCMAAEC logo. I think he was drafting
a reply to a letter the SCMAAEC had sent him.

Letter to the seven county metro area association of emerging churches (SCMAAEC)

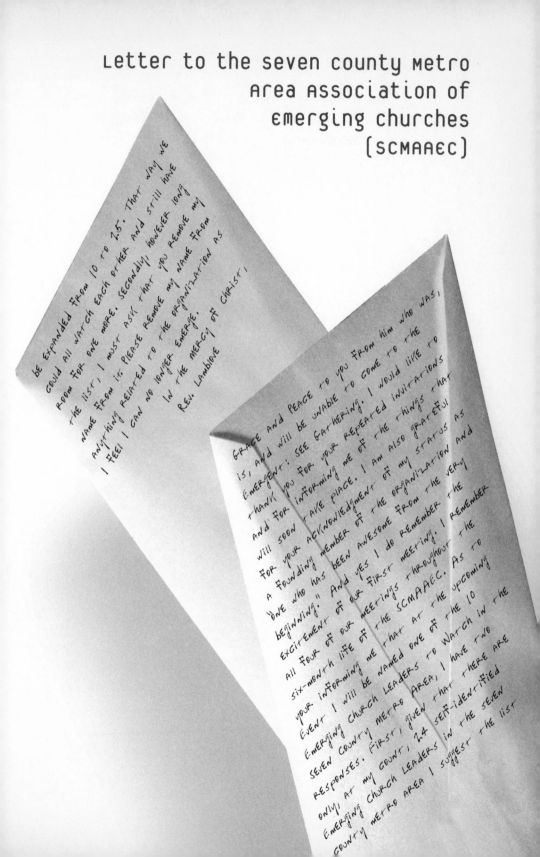

GRACE AND PEACE TO YOU FROM HIM WHO WAS, IS, AND WILL BE UNABLE TO COME TO THE EMERGENT: SEE GATHERING. I WOULD LIKE TO THANK YOU FOR YOUR REPEATED INVITATIONS AND FOR INFORMING ME OF THE THINGS THAT WILL SOON TAKE PLACE. I AM ALSO GRATEFUL FOR YOUR ACKNOWLEDGMENT OF MY STATUS AS A FOUNDING MEMBER OF THE ORGANIZATION AND "ONE WHO HAS BEEN AWESOME FROM THE VERY BEGINNING." AND YES I DO REMEMBER THE EXCITEMENT OF OUR FIRST MEETING. I REMEMBER ALL FOUR OF OUR MEETINGS THROUGHOUT THE SIX-MONTH LIFE OF THE SCMAAEC. AS TO YOUR INFORMING ME THAT AT THE UPCOMING EVENT I WILL BE NAMED ONE OF THE 10 EMERGING CHURCH LEADERS TO WATCH IN THE SEVEN COUNTY METRO AREA, I HAVE TWO RESPONSES. FIRST, GIVEN THAT THERE ARE ONLY, AT MY COUNT, 24 SELF-IDENTIFIED EMERGING CHURCH LEADERS IN THE SEVEN COUNTY METRO AREA I SUGGEST THE LIST BE EXPANDED FROM 10 TO 25. THAT WAY WE COULD ALL WATCH EACH OTHER AND STILL HAVE ROOM FOR ONE MORE. SECONDLY, HOWEVER LONG THE LIST, I MUST ASK THAT YOU REMOVE MY NAME FROM IT. PLEASE REMOVE MY NAME FROM ANYTHING RELATED TO THE ORGANIZATION AS I FEEL I CAN NO LONGER EMERGE.

IN THE MERCY OF CHRIST,
REV. LAMBLOVE

Editor's Comment
....

This early journal entry, along with the note to SCMAAEC, seems to show that Lamblove is breaking decisively with contemporary Christian culture.

journal entry
(Mrs. cheryl johnson)

Mrs. Cheryl Johnson came to my office after the first service yesterday. I've taken to hiding out there almost immediately after the benediction so I don't have to smile and shake too many hands and hear a hundred people say, "Very nice sermon Reverend." It is then all I can do not to squeeze their hand as hard as I can, put my other hand around their throat and say, "Really? What did you like about it? What was it about? What scripture text was it based on? What happened in the last hour? Do you remember, and why do you care?"

Mrs. Johnson wondered if I would mind a little feedback on my preaching. Feedback, I thought. Could she be an octogenarian angel come to lift my spirits? Could she actually have been paying attention all these weeks, applying some yet undemonstrated wisdom of her age? Had she seen my heart turn, following my transformation through my stumbling proclamation? She sees where I want to go and has come to encourage me. Yes, Mrs. Cheryl Johnson, give me feedback!

"I like it when preachers sometimes tell stories. Funny stories."

"Yes?" I said, waiting for her to continue. But that was it.

I decided to tell a funny story. To say what I have been hesitant to say—what I have been trying to prove in my recent exegetical sermons, to say it in a way that might cause Mrs. Johnson to give me some actual response to a sermon.

Editor's Comment

....

This next piece—a sermon—seems to indicate not only a declaration of Lamblove's new-found faith but possibly the beginning of his truly revolutionary proclamations.❋

❋ Of the hundreds of sermons in the box, more than half are directly about or in the persona of a preacher. Why does he write so many sermons about preachers or with preacher characters in them? It seems that he is using his sermons to charge the contemporary Christian culture ministers as the prime culprits in the conspiracy.
He is trying to unmask these contemporary Christian culture conspiracy ministers to the congregation.
This might be a problematic strategy, given that he is the preacher preaching to the C.C.C.C. congregation.

sermon

confessions of a post-evangelical, or jesus in a suitcase

LUKE 10:1–12

After this the Lord appointed seventy others, and sent them on ahead of him, two by two, into every town and place where he himself was about to come. And he said to them, "The harvest is plentiful, but the laborers are few; pray therefore the Lord of the harvest to send out laborers into his harvest. Go your way behold, I send you out as lambs in the midst of wolves. Carry no purse, no bag, no sandals; and salute no one on the road. Whatever house you enter first say, 'Peace be to this house!' And if a son of peace is there, your peace shall rest upon him; but if not, it shall return to you. And remain in the same house, eating and drinking what they provide, for the laborer deserves his wages; do not go from house to house. Whenever you enter a town and they receive you, eat what is set before you; heal the sick in it and say to them, 'The kingdom of God has come near to you.' But whenever you enter a town and they do not receive you, go into its streets and say 'Even the dust of your town that clings to our feet, we wipe off against you; nevertheless know this, that the kingdom of God has come near.' I tell you; it shall be more tolerable on that day for Sodom than for that town.

. . . .

I used to carry Jesus around in a suitcase. I used to take him everywhere I went. Every morning I would get out of bed, put the coffee on, shower, shave, dress. I would take my coffee and Bible into the den, sit down, and pray briefly, "Lord may your Holy Spirit illuminate these words and give me the strength to carry you to the ends of the earth."

I would drink my coffee as fast as I could without burning my mouth in the belief that the more caffeine consumed in the shortest time heightened its bolstering effect.

Next, I would open my Bible to the passages I knew so well, reading them quickly, turning from passage to passage as fast as I could without tearing the pages: "Go into all the world, make disciples, baptizing them in my name." "You will be my witnesses in Jerusalem, Judea, and to the ends of the earth." "The harvest is plentiful, but the laborers are few, therefore ask the Lord of the harvest to send out laborers into his harvest."

And then I would get up and go into the bedroom where I kept Jesus and the suitcase.

I would take the suitcase off the shelf I had built to hold the case and Jesus. The suitcase was a big old black thing made from bonded leather. I bought it at a church rummage sale in Seattle. It was pretty worn, but the hardware was good and the sides and the corners were reinforced, which was what I needed.

I think it must have been used by some sort of traveling salesman. When I got it, the inside was divided into different compartments, like he must have kept his samples in there. I took the dividers out of course. I needed the room.

Near the handle on top, faded gold letters read, "C. K. Milford & Company 1 of 4." Man, I would think sometimes when I saw that, he had to carry four of these things. I don't envy him.

Once I had opened the suitcase on the bed, I would then turn to Jesus. I lifted him off the shelf, careful to lift with my legs and not my back. I would lay the Savior on the bed next to the suitcase and fold him in half at the waist.

Even folded, I had to bend his neck way over to one side to get him to fit in the case. Jesus isn't as big as you'd think, but even so, putting a body in a suitcase is always going to be a tight squeeze. I must admit, though, over time it seemed easier and easier to get him in. I don't know if I just got better at fitting him in or if Jesus got smaller.

After Jesus was packed, I would throw several changes of his clothes in on top. I was the first to do that actually. Believe me or not, but I started the whole dressing-him-up thing. I would take different outfits, depending on which town I was going to be working and what kind of crowd I thought I would encounter. I had a nice charcoal gray business suit; jeans and a tee shirt; a baseball cap (which I have varyingly placed on his head both frontward and backward); the robe of course, the robe—some people still liked to see the robe. I had a western shirt; swimming trunks for summer and ski pants for winter. Never any shoes though. That was always a regret. I just didn't have the room. I'll admit the bare feet did look funny sometimes, especially with that suit.

Then I'd close the suitcase, fastening the clasps carefully to make sure they were secure. As an added precaution, I'd wrap a big strap around the whole thing and cinch it down tight. Then I would haul Jesus down the three flights of stairs from my apartment to the street. I'd put the suitcase in the back seat of my car, and I was off.

I'd show up places, try to find some spot to set up. Sometimes I could get a formal gig—like an Elks Club or a spot at some church's revival meeting. I knew people in some towns who arranged prayer breakfasts or free meals in the park, and I'd work there.

I'd take Jesus out and get him set up and start proclaiming him. I'd preach that the Kingdom of God had come near, give my testimony about how I got Jesus, and then do my darnedest to try to get Jesus into people's hearts. It was hard though, I was always the first to admit. But I guess that's why we're called laborers.

Getting Jesus into people's hearts is harder than carrying him down three flights of stairs. Even if they agree to it—people don't always hold still—they always have this look on their face like they don't completely understand the whole thing. And truth be told, propped up on the street, perhaps in that ski outfit with no shoes on, Jesus didn't exactly cut a striking pose. I'd have to do a lot of talking to convince people he was the savior of the world and could not only relieve their suffering and pain, but guarantee them eternal life.

This went on for years and years. Then some time back, I was in this nondescript farming town up north and things were not going well. I'd had success in the eighties around there with a flannel shirt and feed-cap outfit, but that day nothing was working. I'd given up, shaken the requisite dust off my feet, and was hauling Jesus to my car when two people came out of a coffee shop kind of chuckling pleasantly. I could hear more laughter coming through the door from inside. It just caught me—because, well, it seemed so foreign. I couldn't remember the last time I laughed. I stopped the two guys and asked them, "Excuse me. What's going on in there?"

"Oh, it's just the evangelist," one said as he walked by, still smiling.

"He's a heckuva guy," the other one added.

I was shocked.

It's not that we had territories or anything. It wasn't that. It just seemed so unorthodox—the laughing—his being inside the coffee shop. The whole thing. So I went in. I found a table in the corner, sat down, put the Jesus suitcase on the chair next to me, and watched.

If this man was an evangelist, you couldn't prove it by me. He seemed to know everyone. He would go from one table to another, or people would stop by his table and talk a little, laughing or talking seriously. I sat there through the lunch rush, perplexed. He just seemed to do whatever he wanted and no one seemed to mind. He'd play a song on the jukebox, asking other people what they wanted to hear. He'd go behind the counter, grab the coffeepot, and help out the waitress. I saw him pay two people's checks, and three different people try to pay his.

When the crowd had thinned out, I caught his eye and he came over.

"Hey," he said. "Are you traveling?"

"No. Not exactly. From what I've overheard I think we do the same thing. I'm an evangelist."

"Really?" he said and sat down. "All right—welcome."

"If you don't mind me asking," I said, "um, you seem to know everybody here."

"Well," he said, "I confess, I come in here a lot—great pie."

I was confused, "But you don't, um, have a suitcase."

Now he looked a little confused. "Well, back at the hotel," he said, smiling.

"Well, um . . . where is Jesus?" I asked.

"Oh, he's around here someplace."

"But, don't you carry him . . . with you?"

He laughed like he thought I was joking. Then he could tell I was serious but didn't understand what I meant. "I just go from town to town proclaiming peace to every one of them—the Kingdom of God is here. What a job we have, huh?"

"You come to town without Jesus? How does he get here?"

"Well . . . what do you mean?"

"You don't bring him?" My hand involuntarily grabbed the handle of the suitcase. Now he was looking at me uneasily. "Well if you don't bring him, how do you know he'll come?"

He shook his head, "Are you sure were talking about the same guy?"

"Yeah, Jesus!" I said, shaking the handle of the suitcase.

"What do you have in there?" he asked.

"What, wh-uh-Jesus." I put the suitcase up on the table, opened it, took the clothes off the top and showed him. "What else would I have in the suitcase?"

He was quiet for a minute. Then put his hand on my shoulder and said, "I hate to tell you this, but that's not Jesus."

journal entry
(the spiritual act of shopping)

Dan Wilson stopped me in the parking lot last Sunday to ask about my sermon. He said he stayed for the two o'clock service to hear it again. Which I know meant finding something to do during the Consuming Session between services. (I don't know what they call it these days. Every time a new consultant writes a book with a new bad metaphor for "church growth," the names for everything get changed.) Between the services the people are provided with gracious opportunities to buy things.

Our Senior Pastor explained in one of his weekly "Spelunker's Secrets" all-staff e-mails (it was named during the short time that cave exploring was the dominant metaphor for the New Church Industry. You know, Go Deeper, Bring a Guide, You Can't See Without a Light, It's Dark in Here, Who Grabbed My Ass?) that any church not meeting the Retail Needs of its congregation had an average of only six to thirteen months of "Potential Relevance" left. Potential Relevance is one of the previous Spelunker's Secrets. Once your Potential Relevance numbers dip below three months, you might as well close the doors.

He explained that Retail Needs are like any other needs of an individual. While the eighties finally saw New Churches move beyond the Spiritual Needs of individuals to meet their Gathering Needs and their Convenience Needs, the nineties, he explained, must be remembered as the time when New Churches embraced the whole person by meeting the Retail Needs of the individual.

In a subsection titled The Spiritual Act of Shopping, he summarized his secret. The Contemporary Individual has many and diverse ways of finding and expressing meaning. Buying things is one of the primary means. It is the exchange of our most fluid "meaning place holder" for a more defined "meaning place holder."

People buy things to express themselves and to act out their values. If this is true, then there is an obvious pent-up demand for Contemporary Christian Individuals to express their faith and values in this way. It seems silly, he goes on, that the New Church facilitates people in expressing their Spiritual Needs and their Gathering Needs, but provides no opportunity to express their basic Retail Needs.

People want to buy things at church. People buy all sorts of things to express their other values. They place these items in their homes and on their cars, and they need to be allowed to do the same with their faith. If this need is not being met, seekers will go away unsatisfied and begin to have their Retail Needs met in other, possibly unhealthy, ways.

That is why it is important to make the Purchasing Hour available between services and from 10 A.M. to 9 P.M. weekdays. One can buy any number of things. There are various coffee drinks and pastries. A light lunch can be had. There are stores to buy books and inspirational items and CDs. CDs are big. It is possible to buy CDs of that day's service immediately after the service.

The CDs used to contain the whole service, but now for some reason it is just Our Senior Pastor's introductory sharing thing and the music—all forty-five minutes of the three opening praise songs, the choir, the string quartet, and FoundOut!—the alternative music band (whose name, I was assured when I asked, refers to Jesus finding them, saving them, and their going Out to share his love, and is no way a new ministry to attract homosexual evangelicals, as I had suggested). But the sermons are no longer included.

I asked about it once, and the tech guy said I could order one at the bookstore. When I told the pleasant women behind the counter I wanted to order a sermon CD she laughed and said, "Now why would you want to go and do that? I don't even think they are available. How about 'The Four Powers of Positive Praise'? It comes with a study guide." Then she looked closer, recognized me, and with no effort to try to spare my feelings, gave her little laugh again and said, "Oh, it's you. Now I know why you would want to order a CD. I thought it was kind of a funny request; no one's ever asked before. I don't know if they are available."

I asked her if she could find out if they were available, and she told me that I could go to the bookstore Web site, using one of the Internet stations in the coffee café.

I no longer had the energy to pursue it.

Also, I can guess why they are not available, and in a very small way, it gives me pleasure. I am getting to someone. I am sure that this woman behind the counter was given specific instructions to respond the way she did, down to pretending not to recognize me. Maybe it's not true that people don't ask for them. Maybe many people began to ask for them. Maybe people were saying they just wanted the sermons, wanted a CD without the praise music and Our Senior Pastor's inane self-help-theme-based-topical-introductory-sharing thing—so many that the powers, from the top of the Conspiracy, issued a bookstore policy. I am sure it is actually written down in memo form and taped behind the counter, re-minding employees what to say if someone asks for a sermon CD:

To all employees:

Sermon CDs are not to be sold under any circumstances! If anyone asks be elusive but friendly. Make no definitive statements. Try to get the questioner's name.
—The Management

My sermons are dangerous and it's for that reason they are confiscated after every service. The congregation is beginning to see the light. And the C.C.C.C. cannot afford to let them out of its control. The revolution is building so they must confiscate my weapon. The last thing they would do would be to distribute the very instrument of revolution.

Then again, there might be another reason my sermons are not included on the worship service CDs. It could be related to a presentation Our Senior Pastor gave at NextLeader: A Gathering (I think that is what they were calling the staff meeting then). When I was hired, he introduced me and then went on to explain why he would no longer be preaching. When the title of his PowerPoint presentation jumped up on the screen—Sermons: Are You Sleeping, Brother John?—everyone laughed. I laughed too. I was happy to have this job. I longed for this kind of relevant, even edgy, critique. And I was excited that Our Senior Pastor had turned over his preaching duties to me. He knew I was young and on fire for the Lord and could relate to the young congregation.

By that time, I had already been experimenting a bit with the form of the sermon. I thought this forward-thinking church (it was rated in the top ten New Thinking New Churches in 1997) would challenge me to go further. I guess I wasn't yet aware to what extent and in what direction. At the time I was flattered, and in the time of the Pioneer metaphor, truly considered myself a Brush Clearer and not a Sod Buster (although I acknowledged both were needed).

Naturally, I was taken aback when he went on to show through charts and graphs and bullet points that the sermon was old technology and tested below "the prayer of dismissal" for positive response. Therefore as the Lead Wrangler, it would border on *causing a brother to stumble* if he still endorsed or in any way identified himself with this dead and outdated element of worship. And even though there had never been a sermon in the earliest

Christian services of worship,❇ many still thought of it as essential, even if they never paid attention, so it would be kept in until appropriate "transitional preparations" could be made.

The sermon, he said, would be moved to the very end so the worship experience could be front-loaded. Instead of preaching, he would give brief, biblically influenced insights and learnings. "And then," he said, gesturing to me, "our new Vice President for Preaching and Biblical Study will give the remaining few what they think they need."

The change was met with near-universal enthusiasm. There was even an article in the on-line version of Re:Church, hailing the move as the next necessary element in worship restructuring.

Knowing that Dan Wilson would even listen to my sermon, not to mention stay to hear it twice, gave me much-needed energy to continue the Revolution.

He asked me, in reference to the sermon, "Are both parts true?"

"I think so," I told him.

I like that Dan Wilson.

❇ Not that I need to fight Lamblove's battles, but it is hard to let this statement go. Granted this is Lamblove reporting that His Senior Pastor said there were no sermons in the earliest whorship (why do I always misspell *worship* "whorship"?) services; still, it should be corrected. My reading of church history and the book of Acts finds the sermon along with the Eucharist as the center point of the whorship service.

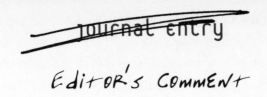

~~Journal Entry~~

Editor's Comment

I woke up this morning (11:00 A.M. is still the morning) on my living room floor in a pile of Lamblove's papers, my mouth thick and pasty, mind about the same. It is a good thing I don't have much of a job. The Reverend has been keeping me up late.

In struggling to put together these writings in some semblance of chronology, I find myself looking for hints of his personal life in his sermons. I don't know if his sermons reflect his life in the church and his relationships with his colleagues; I don't want to read in what is not there. I have only the sparsest material, so I cannot resist when I find a possible reference.

But then I think of Jim Larson, this painter I kind of know. I was looking at one of his paintings. It was like a meadow or something. I was trying to appear to be an astute observer of art, so I pointed out that I could see the face he had subtly hidden in the swirls of grass. He said that he hadn't hidden a face in the grass but that you could find a face in anything. If you look at the clouds or a water stain on the ceiling or a mountain, you can usually find something that looks like a face, because at the back of our minds that's what we are always looking for.

I am afraid that is what I am doing with Rev. Lamblove's sermons. I don't know his face. I don't really know who he is. A box of crazy, semi-interesting writings is not quite as interesting without a face. I want to find the life behind the things in this box. But like I said, I don't really have that much to go on. When I started this project I was simply going to collect his sermons. The whole thing was going to be about preaching. Then I realized some of his other random notes gave some insight into the sermons. Then I became obsessed with his life and the shape of his soul, but I didn't have any real biographical information. So now I have something that is neither a collection of sermons nor a biography. It is admittedly a mess. I think of it as sort of an iceberg biography. I can only provide you, dear reader, with the ten percent of his life that sticks above the water. The other ninety must be filled in by your own speculation.

journal entry
(I don't know about technology)

I don't know much about technology, but I think someone did something to my car radio. I will even go so far as to say someone tampered with it. It is not broken. It just doesn't work like it is supposed to.

I discovered this on my way to work. My car was going really fast, too fast. Which is another odd thing because my car doesn't usually go fast on the way to work, especially on a Monday after I've preached. But this morning it was going fast and I noticed this, and my noticing made me think of a song that made me think of the general category of songs that brought to mind my car radio. So I turned it on. I could tell almost immediately that something was wrong. (I did not suspect tampering right away.)

The radio turns on but you can't hear the sound. It is not that the sound isn't coming out, because it is. I can tell the sound is coming out. I just can't hear it.

I wonder if someone who knows about technology or electronics can do some high-tech thing to make it so a sound exists but no one can hear it. It seems possible. It must be possible. I know it is. There can be no other explanation.

I have been thinking about this since this morning. After my silent drive to work, I had an experience in the church office that got me thinking about the device that might cause this. It must be a kind of sound canceller—something that can generate the exact opposite sound waves, thereby canceling out the sound. I don't know if there is such a thing. It is more technology and I don't know about technology. But if there is such a thing, I am wondering if it has been put into use when I preach. Amy, a Support Team member, tipped me off, and I don't think it was accidental.

I went into the office, which I can barely bring myself to do, to pick up my mail and Sunday's response cards. Response cards are put in every worship folder (that's what they call the Sunday bulletin), so the congregation can share what they valued about their worship experience directly with the Leadership Team. "Think of them as customer satisfaction reports," Our Senior Pastor said.

I had not been to the office to pick up my mail or to check on how satisfied the customers are in over a month. It is too anxiety-producing. I never know who is going to be in there. Sometimes it is just Support Team members. But other times the office is filled with every kind of Coach, Wrangler, Navigator, and VP imaginable. I don't even know what everyone on the Leadership Team does, but talking to them makes my ears ring and my mind jump around. I can't think of what words to say, so I usually prepare something to say before I go in the office just in case I have to speak. I try to find something that can be both an answer to an inquiry and a greeting. I realize sometimes I need to talk first if someone looks at me. Sometimes I say, "Full sail." People seem to like this. When I enter the office and the Lead Coach for Vision Tracking or someone like that is standing by the mailboxes, I can say, "Full sail?" to which he will likely reply, "Up and running," or something to indicate his general state of satisfaction and determination. If he speaks first and says, for instance, "How goes it?" I can reply, "Full sail." Before I reached the office today, I decided on "Forward ho." "Forward ho?" "Forward ho!" Yes, it works.

I try to walk in the office with a casual joviality, which I affect by tilting my head slightly back and to the left and swinging my right arm broadly.

I walk into the office. "Forward ho?!" I say this as I swing my arm. Amy, the Support Team member, is sorting the mail.

"Forward ho," she says, smiling. I look in my mailbox. It is empty. All the other Team Leaders' boxes seemed to be stuffed with response cards. Amy sees me looking in the box. She takes a blank response card, writes something on it, looks me in the eye (purposefully?), and puts it in my box. I take it out and put it in the outside pocket of my bag.

When I get to my office, I shut the door and look around the room. I sit down. How is it possible that I have gotten no response to my "Jesus in a Suitcase" sermon? I pulled back the veil, shined the light on the heart of the conspiracy. And not one response. Well, I guess one. I pull Amy's card out of my bag. It says, "I wish I could have heard you on Sunday." It is confirmed. The device was definitely in place. She could not hear me. She could not hear me. This would explain the blank looks on the faces in the congregation. I am sure she could not risk saying anything more. I will try another time to find out what she knows.

Editor's Comment

....

Evidently, Lamblove had a series of dreams or visions that he recorded in his journal as "post-apocalyptic." I have included three. I have left out the more disturbing ones and, truthfully, some of the more embarrassing ones. What I cannot tell is whether these vision/dreams are the source of his ideas about the Contemporary Christian Culture Conspiracy or they are his own conscious creation. Is he placing his ideas about the conspiracy in the context of a vision to avoid taking responsibility for his outlandish speculation or to appear less nuts?

Post-Apocalyptic Praise Song,
Part One

I don't want to scare anyone. I just want to get this down. I feel like somewhere someone told me to write what I have been shown. Shown? I don't even know how I know what I know. I don't know if it was a dream I had and can't remember, or if it was a dream someone else had and forgot. All I know is that it was all about that song. Everybody was supposed to sing the song, but I don't think anybody did. Well, some people might have tried to, but they couldn't convince themselves enough that the world had ended, so they just tried to sing it and then stopped.

In this dream, or vision . . . (Is it too much to say vision? It seems like a vision. Vision is too much—I'll say dream.) In this dream it was the end of the world. Well, it might have been the end of the world, or at least it was supposed to be. Everyone wanted it to be over, but it just wasn't and it put everyone in such a bad mood.

I know this sounds weird. I will just tell you what I saw as I was standing in the rain, at night, in the middle of the street. (Maybe it wasn't rain. It must have been more like a light sleet. Because I wasn't getting soaked but it made me squint.) Anyway, I looked up the street and down the street and in both directions I saw strip malls: one per block, the same on each side of the street, identical and repeating, block after block. They were set back from the street with plenty of parking in front. They each contained what looked to be an off-brand convenience store (not 7-Eleven or SuperAmerica) and a video store with a huge sign in the window that said

All the Latest Titles All the Time—No Waiting

And another one said

Can't Decide? Let Us Choose for You!

Next to the video store was a dry cleaner, then a computer store, and then a bookstore.

We're standing in the rain (or this light sleet), in the middle of the street; he is looking one way, and I am looking the other. Then I look one way and he looks the other. (Oh yeah, I forgot to mention, there's this guy in this part. You know how dreams are: sometimes he's there and sometimes it's just me.)

So I'm standing there and I am watching. Up and down each block as far as I can see, cars are pulling into the strip malls, and people are going into all the stores. All of these places are doing brisk business—cars going in and out of the parking lots, people going in and out of every store on every block.

As we continue to watch, I notice something odd.

I see someone walk into the video store with an armload of dirty shirts. He drops them off and comes out with his dry-cleaning ticket. Then I see someone else come out of the video store with her dry cleaning. And someone goes in, then comes out of the convenience store with a bag from the bookstore. Another person comes out of the computer store with a carton of milk.

The stores people went into seemed to be a random decision dictated, as far as I could tell, by whatever store was closest to where they were parked.

Then I noticed that every store had the same sticker on the door, announcing that they were a "C4! Store."

C4? The guy just looked at me. C4?

"I don't know," I said.

He tapped me on the shoulder and pointed up to the big, lighted sign in the corner of the parking lot. I looked down the street and for the first time saw the signs on every strip mall on every block, brightly lit and turning slowly:

C4! Contemporary Christian Convenience Center

It was only then that I became aware of the traffic whipping by me in both directions, barely missing me, cars throwing off light sleet from their big tires.

I was starting to have trouble catching my breath. I couldn't really swallow. Contemporary Christian Convenience Center?

Then I saw it. That wasn't a real bookstore. It was a Christian Bookstore. I could see the best-seller list posted in the window with a headline over it, reading:

Number One 14 Years in a Row
What Would Jesus Do?—The Video Game!

The dry cleaner was called White as Snow. Every car in the parking lot was the same: huge sport utility vehicles with the fish symbol on the back.

I heard tires screeching, and an old minivan slammed to a stop right in front of us. The side door slid open, two people grabbed me, threw me inside, and sped away. The next thing I remember, we are parked in the parking lot of an abandoned convenience store on a side street. I am sitting on the curb in front of the store, two guys are sitting on either side of me, and a couple of other people are pacing back and forth. One of them—a woman—stops and shoves the piece of paper in my face. "Have you ever seen this before?"

It is a piece of paper with *the song* on it. I could tell by the way the letters were distorted that it had been photocopied over and over again. I told her I never had—because even though I did know what it was, I only knew in a dream sort of way, not in a real way.

"What is going on . . . ?" I started to say. "This is all so weird."

Then they told me what was going on. And this next part—I don't think it is part of the dream.

You see, things had gone quite well for the Contemporary Christians. Their message had been nearly universally accepted, and what was once referred to as American Culture was now commonly known as Contemporary Christian Culture. What was once seen as Western capitalism was now known as Contemporary Christian Capitalism. The markets thrived, the economy thrived, every kind of thing that could thrive, thrived. You could get anything you wanted at the local C4! Store. It was so convenient, and it was helping other people when you bought things. It wasn't even called buying anymore. It was called a Praise Exchange, because everybody was just so happy to have been blessed with so much, and they were all so happy to be getting more.

Everyone was, as they liked to say, of one accord. Everything was so peaceful; things were so nice and convenient. It was a good comfortable life.

Everyone had been working together on "the Commission." (You know, the great commission, the one from the end of Matthew's gospel.) Everyone just referred to it as the Commission. It was overseen by the Commission Commission. People would say to one another in the break room at work, "Have you heard how the Commission is going this week?" Or, "Did you see the Commission on Oprah yesterday?" or "Did you hear the Commission finished up Micronesia?"

You see, Matthew's great commission commanded the followers of Jesus to go to all the world baptizing and making disciples. The Commission Commission understood this to mean that the Contemporary Christians must present the plan of salvation to every last person on earth. (Every last person on earth did not have to accept Jesus as their personal lord and savior. They only had to have been presented with the plan of salvation.) When every last person on earth had heard the Four Spiritual Laws, the Romans Road, the Glory Guide, then Jesus would return. The End of the

Age would be upon us—the end of the world as we know it. Jesus would return on a cloud.

As the reports grew more and more favorable, it became clear that in the not-too-distant future the Commission was going to be complete. I mean, if you want something done, ask a Contemporary Christian. (You want to talk about control and organization? The whole culture was Type A.) Not only did they get things done, but they were thoughtful. So they started thinking, "You know, if the end of the world is coming and Jesus is going to return, don't you think it would be nice to welcome him somehow? You know, make him feel comfortable?"

Inspired by this goodwill, the Commission Commission commissioned a song—a praise song—for everyone to sing. The idea was that after the last person had received Heaven's Handshake, heard the Sinner's Serenade, and the Commission was complete, everyone throughout the world would simultaneously sing this praise song and that would be Jesus' cue to return.

But things didn't work out the way the Commission planned.

When the last person on earth had heard the Glory Guide, there was a big announcement so everyone knew the last person had been witnessed to. Really, if everyone was being honest and following the rules, the song should have been sung. People started singing, but, well, frankly stated, Jesus did not return so they just kind of stopped.

This is the great apocalypse? The sound of a praise song petering out? Where was the Last Trumpet's sound, the peals of thunder? In some sectors the song was started with bravado and in others with the enthusiasm of an embarrassed kid being forced to play her violin for visitors. While they sang everyone was looking, but no one saw a thing. Looking up—no hail mixed with fire. Looking down—no earth opening up and swallowing the evildoers. Looking around—no beast with a mortal wound that had healed; no seven-headed monster; not even a two-headed calf or a lobster boy. The whole thing lost steam. Throughout the world there was only mumbling, then just feet shuffling, and the occasional clearing of a throat.

What happened? One could only think:

A. We missed some people. (There was the debate about whether statistical sampling was more accurate or whether an actual count should have been used.) Or
B. God left us hanging. Or
C. We told everybody the wrong thing. We somehow messed up the Good News. All that witnessing and people had unashamedly been proclaiming the wrong thing.

Whatever speculations the Contemporary Christians might have been making, the people who kidnapped us in the minivan and brought us to the abandoned convenience store said the world didn't end because when the Contemporary Christians were out boldly proclaiming the Good News of the Kingdom of God, they were proclaiming the wrong thing. And all you had to do was compare the Commission's Contemporary Christian Proclamation Pamphlet with what it says in the Bible and you would see.

I told them they were wrong, that they were liars and probably would not know the Good News if they were beaten with it. I grabbed up the photocopy of the song they showed me, and we made a break for it.

The guy who was with me saw that the keys were in the minivan and jumped in the driver's seat. I jumped in the side door, and we took off. I told him to drive to the nearest, biggest church he could find, and we would get to the bottom of this.

So. I am in the back of the old minivan, rolling around with every turn and swerve because there are no seats in the back and that guy is driving really fast, which I told him to do, but he seems like he would be a bad driver even if he were going slow. This guy, he doesn't say much, and when he does it doesn't make much sense. Really, he seems like kind of an idiot. But he smiles like he seems happy (which, given the situation, makes him seem like even more of an idiot). He turns a corner, hits the curb; I roll and catch my right ear on the door handle. I call him an idiot. He smiles and says his name is John. I don't know how Idiot John came to be with me in my vision dream thing, and even though he is an idiot I am glad to have him along. It is nice to have company in a vision of the end of the world.

We see what looks like a giant shopping mall off in the distance. I tell Idiot John to head for it. That is what we are looking for. As we approach, there is a sign directing us various places under the name in clean, but progressive-looking, italicized letters: *PraiseWind Contemporary Christian Campus Center*. Arrows point in different directions to the café, bookstore, stables (stables?); it is hard to read as we fly by so quickly. We obviously made a wrong turn, followed the wrong arrow. I figured we should go directly to the church, where they actually had church services, but it was hard to tell from the sign where that was, and we end up around the back of the enormous complex by all the dumpsters. We had followed a sign that said Service Entrance. It was an easy mistake. Without slowing down, Idiot John made a U-turn back to the main entrance, and we followed another arrow and slammed to a stop in the only empty space among acres of cars. I got out and stood on the bumper of the minivan to see if I could spot the actual church part of the Church Campus Center thing. A sign on a light pole indicated that we were in the Jude section of the lot, so the church had to be a ways away.

A black SUV appeared out of nowhere and parked crossways behind us. A professional-sports-player-sized man stepped quickly from the driver's side (you know the kind of professional sports guy who becomes a born-again Contemporary Christian and then starts sucking at his professional sport). He stood there solidly and smiled pleasantly. I jumped down off the bumper. Idiot John stuck his head out the window and smiled back at the professional sports guy.

He seems very friendly. He is wearing a dark suit with a kind of a badge on the breast pocket that says, "Usher." He begins to speak to us in a very friendly, casual way, explaining that he would have to detain us while he runs a security check on our police records. (I thought at church we could figure everything out. But the minivan—it was our downfall. The professional sports guy said the minivan is a problem, because nobody drives them anymore but poor people and criminals.)

That is what he said. Apparently, he explained as he pulled Idiot John out of the van, back in the 1990s so many people bought minivans, and then, a couple years later, replaced them with brand new sport utility vehicles. Suddenly there were all these practically-brand-new minivans on the market, and within a few short months there were so many that not only could you not sell them, you could not even give them away.

This whole time he is twisting our arms behind our backs and putting us in the back, caged part of this huge SUV, he is talking calmly, even pleasantly.

"We thought," he went on, "since we can't sell them, we should give them to the needy." Which is, of course, what you do with anything you grow tired of, is out of fashion, ugly, useless, and cannot be turned into money; anything you cannot bear to have around but can't think of a good way to get rid of. You give it to the needy. (That is what Idiot John said to the guy. I kicked him in the shin to shut him up. But the guy didn't seem to mind. It didn't even faze him.)

"Well," he says, "it might seem no good to us, but the needy are different."

"They have less stuff," Idiot John says, smiling. (I was starting to think that he was going to get us in trouble.)

"To deal with the problem, the Elder Board of the Department of Transportation and Safety instituted a program intended to distribute minivans to the needy, but it was a hassle. Because the minivans had no value, they weren't deductible. So people figured the needy would just take them if they really needed them. People would sign the titles, place them on the dashboard with the keys, and leave the minivans parked on the streets or in the parking lots of the Convenience Centers."

I couldn't really keep track of where he was driving us, but I figured it was somewhere around another side of the Campus Center Mall Church place. He backed up to a door and came around and let us out. The door opened and he indicated that we should go in first. "Thank you," Idiot John said. The usher kept talking as he directed us through these fluorescent-lit, institutional-tile-covered hallways.

"These abandoned minivans were everywhere. It became such a public nuisance that no one who had a choice would be seen in a minivan, because you were guilty by association." As if by driving one you were somehow related to or responsible for all these abandoned minivans. You would hear people comment as they drove past a particularly large cluster of abandoned minivans, "Why don't those people clean up their own mess?" (As if the person making the comment hadn't dumped a minivan or two somewhere.)

"Anyway," the guy said, as he was locking us in this kind of holding room, "that's why we have to hold you for a while. Just to check things out. We usually don't have any minivans in the parking lot; we don't allow them, frankly. Someone might be trying to abandon it."

I.J. started up again: "What if someone driving a minivan wants to come to church?"

The guy smiled and said, "I'll just check some things out and be back." And he leaves us in the holding room. I am scared. Why would they put us in here? Why does a church even have a holding room?

And this is where I get really scared, because I look closer, and Idiot John is looking at me so strangely. Because Idiot John is not Idiot John anymore. He is someone else, a person I have never seen before. Then he tells me (not *him*, but the person that he's become) tells me: "Jesus did not come into this world to bring peace but a sword. Let's be clear about the context here. Jesus is giving instructions to his disciples and sending them out on a mission. He is telling them to go proclaim this good news: The Kingdom of Heaven has come near. Who should hear the Good News?

Jesus says, Don't go anywhere near those sinners, those gentiles and Samaritans. Don't go around any neighborhoods where those other folks live. No, no, no. Go first to the house of Israel, to the insiders, to our folks. Jesus said you have to go to our folks first and try to get them to understand.

❯ ❯ ❯ ❯ ❯ ❯ ❯

Peace. What is peace? This *peace* that Jesus is talking about is what we would probably call *convenience*. There is no peace. Only convenience."

post-Rapture Radio
part two

judgment and
Armageddon

from Lamblove's commentary on the Book of Revelation

Nothing but the Blood of Jesus

There is blood all over the book of Revelation. All kinds of blood. The saints wash their robes in the blood of the Lamb. Blood mixed with fire is hurtled to the ground. Blood conquers Satan. John covers the book in blood, covers the world in blood. Blood is Judgment.

In chapter 14, verses 19 and 20, John reports, "So the angel swung his sickle on the earth and gathered the vintage of the earth, and threw it in to the great wine press of the wrath of God; and the wine press was trodden outside the city, and blood flowed from the wine press, as high as a horse's bridle for one thousand six hundred stadia." (RSV)

This is serious judgment.

In chapter 16, verses 4 through 6, John tells us, "The third angel poured his bowl into the rivers and the fountains of water and they became blood. I heard the angel of water say, 'Just art thou in these thy judgments, thou who art and wast, O Holy One. For men have shed the blood of the saints and prophets, and thou hast given them blood to drink. It is their due!'" (RSV)

Blood is mercy.

It is remarkable how John weaves the judgment of all and the salvation of all throughout the book. The verses cited are particularly odd and beautiful. He transforms the wine into blood and the blood into the Eucharist. The blood that flows from the wine press

of God's wrath outside the city is a reference to Jesus being crucified outside the city (as the gospels tell us he was), and as a result
that blood is offered to those who have shed the blood of the
saints. This blood is the new covenant, which God makes with us
for the forgiveness of sin (as the gospels put it).

Judgment and mercy mix like blood and water.

sermon

A Good Televangelist Is Hard to Find

MATTHEW 4:1–11

Then Jesus was led up by the Spirit into the wilderness to be tempted by the devil. He fasted forty days and forty nights, and afterwards he was famished. The tempter came and said to him, "If you are the Son of God, command these stones to become loaves of bread." But he answered, "It is written, one does not live by bread alone, but by every word that comes from the mouth of God."

Then the devil took him to the holy city and placed him on the pinnacle of the temple, saying to him, "If you are the Son of God, throw yourself down; for it is written, 'He will command his angels concerning you. And on their hands they will bear you up, so that you will not dash your foot against a stone.'" Jesus said to him, "Again it is written, do not put the Lord your God to the test."

Again, the devil took him to a very high mountain and showed him all the kingdoms of the world and their splendor; and he said to him, "All these I will give you, if you will fall down and worship me." Jesus said to him, "Away with you, Satan! For it is written, worship the Lord your God and serve only him."

Then the devil left him, and suddenly angels came and waited on him.

. . . .

There is a very interesting story attached to this section of scripture. I don't know if you remember the great wave of televangelist scandals of the eighties, or perhaps read about them in your history class in high school. But anyway, this text, Matthew 4:1–11, commonly known as the Temptation of Jesus (although, I must say, a somewhat misleading title), was responsible for making and destroying one of the greatest of the early eighties televangelists.

His name was the Rev. Major Dawn (which was, I must say, a somewhat misleading name). The Rev. Major Dawn had built an international evangelism empire. He had a huge world headquarters in Orlando, Florida; he had a television studio with satellite uplinks, a publishing company, his own brand of salsa. He had everything.

But it all came crashing down when he was discovered in Laughlin, Nevada, passed out in a hotel room with a frog and an antelope in the room.

It was one of those situations you can't recover from. He lost everything. The police arrested him but couldn't really figure out what to charge him with. Then it was discovered that the frog was an endangered species, so he pled guilty to a lesser charge in a plea bargain and was given two hundred hours of community service in the reptile house at the Reno Zoo.

But the interesting part of the story is how the Rev. Major Dawn came to be a televangelist at all. He was once a well-respected, ordinary pastor of a local church. It was this text that started the whole fiasco. He was preparing for a sermon on temptation titled, "Don't Give In or You Won't Get In," when he had what he considered to be a profound insight into the text. If you will indulge me, I will lay it out for you briefly.

In the first chapter of Matthew's gospel, in referring to the birth of the Messiah, Matthew quotes Isaiah saying, "All this took place to fulfill what had been spoken by the Lord through the prophet, 'Look a virgin shall conceive and bear a son and they shall name him Emmanuel,' which means, 'God with us.'"

This notion that Jesus is Emmanuel—God with us—becomes the central theme of Matthew's gospel. With that theme in mind, Rev. Dawn reads the temptation story and realizes that the word usually translated "tempting" is more accurately translated "testing," which would be consistent with the word used for "the devil," which means "tester."

So the beginning of chapter 4 now sounds a little different. "Then Jesus was led up by the Spirit into the wilderness to be tested by the tester." It sounds a little bit like the book of Deuteronomy, when Israel cries out to God, "Have you led us out into the wilderness to test us?"

Furthermore, he realizes that the entire situation echoes Deuteronomy chapters 6 and 8 (this, of course, through no cleverness of his own, because it says as much in the footnotes of his Bible).

In Jesus' first test the devil says, "If you are the Son of God then turn these stones into bread." Jesus answers by saying, "One does not live by bread alone, but by every word that proceeds from the mouth of God."

In Deuteronomy, Moses says that God tested Israel in the wilderness, giving them nothing to eat but manna so that they would learn that one does not live by bread alone, but by every word that proceeds from the mouth of God.

In Jesus' second test in the wilderness, the devil brings Jesus to the pinnacle of the temple and says, "If you are the Son of God, throw yourself off for it is written, 'He will command his angels concerning you, on their hands they will bear you up, that you will not dash your food on a stone.'"

Jesus replies, "It is also written, 'You should not put the Lord your God to the test.'"

Where is it written? Of course, in Deuteronomy.

In the third and final test, the devil takes Jesus to a high hill overlooking all the kingdoms of the world and says, "All this will be yours if you only bow down and worship me."

Jesus replies, "Away with you Satan, for it is written, 'Worship the Lord your God and serve him only.'"

This of course echoes the situation in Deuteronomy where Moses has led Israel to a hill overlooking the promised land and reminds them of God's commandment to love the Lord their God with all their heart and with all their soul and with all their might, and that if they worship the Lord their God and serve him, only *they* will live long and prosper in the land.

So, in seeing this relationship between Jesus being tested in the wilderness and Israel being testing in the wilderness, Rev. Dawn realizes that Matthew has begun to make good on his claim that Jesus is "God with us" by literally placing Jesus with Israel at the most vulnerable and desperate part of their history.

And agreeing with most scholars that Matthew was written for a Jewish audience, he saw then that Matthew was making the claim that Jesus did not come to replace Israel (as God's chosen people) with gentiles but came to be with Israel in fulfilling God's plan for them that they be a witness to all nations.

Furthermore (and I am sorry for going on and on. This is the final point in Rev. Major's exegesis, and then I promise I will get back to recounting the amusing downfall of a once-powerful man) . . . furthermore, he realized that all the tests the devil gave Jesus in the wilderness were designed to get Jesus to separate himself from God and to proceed without God.

All the things the devil asked Jesus to do would have benefited his mission, proving beyond the shadow of a doubt that he was who he said he was: the Son of God—like a public display of his power, throwing himself off the top of the temple and having the angels save him, right in the middle of the city where everyone could see. Certainly people would follow him after they saw his power. And finally, all the kingdoms of the world could be his. He could rule them all as the Kingdom of God.

But all these things would require Jesus to do one thing. He would have to sever his relationship with God.

Rev. Dawn thought that this was the greatest test of all. It is, in fact, the failure of this test that is Original Sin. Above all else, God desires relationship with God's children and secondly desires that God's children be in relationship with each other.

Sin, Rev. Dawn said, is the breaking of that relationship. Some action might not be wrong or bad or sinful in itself; it only becomes sin if it breaks one's relationship with God or one's neighbor.

He reasoned that if God's desire is to be with us (which is made definitive in Jesus, Emanuel, God-with-us), the greatest temptation is to break that "with-ness."

And it was that phrase that launched his empire.

He found that he could avoid all the baggage of the guilt and shame of American pietism by simply talking about God's desire to be with us, in relationship. And individuals should strive not for perfection, or morality, but instead to be in relationship with God and their fellows. And people could simply ask themselves how any thought or deed would affect their being with—in relationship with—God or their fellows. And if a thought or deed broke that with-ness, people should avoid it, or if harm was already done, they should seek to repair the relationship right away. He called this the With-ness Test.

He wrote a book of the same name; it was a best-seller in the early eighties. He went on to speak all over the world. He would start every crusade meeting by shouting out, "Can I get a with-ness?" and encourage people to go "with-nessing." At first it sounded to some as if he had a lisp, but his with-nessing movement grew. It was especially popular in certain parts of Spain.

As the years went on, he wrote more and more books, selling them and all kinds of other with-ness paraphernalia through his daily TV show.

Then one day he was with an architect looking at the site of the new mega-worship tabernacle, and the architect commented on what a great site it was up on this hill. "You can look out over your entire compound. Wow," he said. "It's all yours as far as the eye can see."

And that is what led to his breakdown. "All mine," he thought, "mine alone." He became crazed and completely self-indulgent, thinking he was the arbiter of all that was good and right. And it was this arrogant depravity that finally led him to be discovered in that hotel in Laughlin, Nevada.

In an interview some years later, he said that was the best thing that ever happened to him. It humbled him and reminded him what he was so passionate about in the first place. But alas, shortly after that he moved to the Castilian region of Spain and rebuilt his empire.

He would have been a good man if he'd had an antelope and frog there to humble him every day of his life.❋

❋ Am I reading between the lines too much here, or is this a direct attack on His Senior Pastor?

journal entry
(Address to the
Maple Lakes Rotary Club)*

I am beginning to think that they know what I am thinking. I was asked by Pastor Bob (who received a memo from Pastor Dale, who had a meeting with Our Senior Pastor) to give an address to the Maple Lakes Rotary Club on the topic "Reading the Bible Today."

Supposedly, Mr. Breadeson, the chair of the speakers committee for the MLRC, who is also the director of the church's "Prayer in the Schools: After-School" program made the request for Our Senior Pastor specifically. Our Senior Pastor, however, thought "it was a better fit" for me, according to Pastor Dale's memo to Pastor Bob. So Bob tells me. I guess Mr. Breadeson thought that being director of the PS:AS carried a little more weight than it does. But one look at the organizational chart would have tempered his hubris. The PS:AS is not even a Ministry. It is not even a Focus. It is certainly not a Ministry Focus. On the Organizational Map, to find Mr. Breadeson's directorship one has to start with the 7 Values and follow the branch under A People Interactive to the 4 Interactions of an Interactive People. There under the branch of Re:Claiming one finds 5 Focuses (Foci?). Focus 4 is Education, and under Education Focus are the Ministry Branches, and under each of those are their related Ministry Focuses, and under the Ministry Focuses are the Ministry Focuses in Action. The PS:AS is merely a Ministry Focus in Action, and

---

* I found this in a note titled "Ideas for Maple Lakes Rotary Club Address," written on both sides of a driver's license renewal form and concluding on the cover of a brochure declaring, "Mold, Mildew, and Dust: Enemy of the Older Home."

frankly this request should have been passed on to a Partnering Pastor (which means Sunday school teacher).

That this request was so pointedly given to me from the top must certainly mean something. I think it is a warning, a reminder of my status, that I should remember that I am a Box Car and not an Engine or a Caboose.❇

But that was not my first reaction when it was all explained to me, in the most honorific language, by Pastor Bob. My first reaction was, "There are still Rotary Clubs? That is a real thing?" I have only heard about this kind of thing from old guys I would visit in the hospital when I did my chaplaincy internship in seminary.

My second thought was, "They want me to give an address? What is an address?" Bob said it is just a talk or a speech. But an address is not a talk or a speech; an address is a location. They want me to give a location—a location of "Reading the Bible Today." And I bet they want the address to be some place they have been before.

So I found an address: the location of the heart of the whole thing.

This is what I told the Maple Lake Rotary Club while they sat eating their eggs and toast in the Denny's Banquet and Meeting Room with its acoustic tile ceiling and its broad windows looking out on the freeway off-ramp:

Everyone who reads the Bible brings to it assumptions or methods which they use to interpret the meaning of what they are reading. This is called hermeneutics. The Contemporary Christian Church has a very distinct way of interpreting the Bible. I call this the Evan-

❇ This seemingly enigmatic reference is somewhat clarified by an undated journal entry commenting on a children's sermon given by another leader in which he explains it received more response than his "Adult Sermon" that followed. His sermon was called, "Teleology as a Negation of the Experiential." The children's sermon was called, "Thomas the Train: Discipleship for Young People."

gelical Hermeneutic. It is what keeps the Contemporary Christian Culture Cancer growing, and the Contemporary Christian unwittingly brings this disease, as insidious as an undiagnosed leukemia, to the text. For once deep inside the conspiracy, it is impossible to see a biblical passage any other way. The cancer cannot be removed. The patient must be removed, and that only by death.

When approaching a text, such a person unconsciously applies the following principles to find its meaning.

- It is about me. Whatever the book, be it Pentateuch, prophets, psalms, gospel, or epistle, it is talking about me.
- It tells me what to do or what not to do. An action is required on my part. My ability to do or not to do what the Bible tells me is equal to my goodness or wickedness.
- It condemns those who are different from me, that is, people who are non-Christian (those who freely admit their lack of faith or, what's worse, profess a false faith) or un-Christian (people who say they are Christian but demonstrate their lack of salvation by their actions, whether it be thinking premarital sex is not bad or going to an Episcopal church).
- It implies the opposite. Every pronouncement of grace points to my own condemnation if I fail. Every promise is a threat. Everything that God does reveals what I must do.

These guiding principles of the Evangelical Hermeneutic stem from the original misspelled DNA of the cancer: the Evangelical Fallacy. The Evangelical Fallacy is the bastardization of a logical equation that is never allowed to be resolved. Its resolution would overcome the Contemporary Christian and reveal their God to be the monster he is and confirm their own long-suspected but unconsciously hidden conviction that they are doomed, that they will not die but will live in everlasting torture assigned to them by the gleeful, dripping jaws of a sadistic God who snarls endlessly, "I told you so. I warned you."

The logical equation that is written in the DNA of the Contemporary Christian is simple:

If A and B then C.

But in practice, it is always and must always be

If A and B then . . .

The equation is never—and must never be—resolved.

If A. God will love you and save you if you are good.

And B. You are a sinner and can never be good.

Then C. God will never love you and save you.

It is remarkable that someone growing up in the Contemporary Christian Culture can hear the same Bible stories and have them interpreted in Sunday school, Vacation Bible school, Youth Group, Summer Camp, Youth for Christ, Young Adult Studies, Adult Sunday school, Bible Studies, Retreats and Sermons—and hear the same thing said about the same verses *every time.*

There is no significant variation. A story might start out being told by puppets and flannel graphs, and end up being told with acoustic guitars, and finally by boring or exuberant white men. But it is always the same. Over time, nearly every text is covered.

Like a vaccine, these interpretations contain just a little bit of the truth and are given over time until the hearer is inoculated against being infected by the Good News in any text.

By the time a Contemporary Christian is an adult, any one of them could teach a Bible Study or lead a Youth Group or preach a sermon. They have absorbed the Contemporary Christian Culture reading of the text. A person might not even remember studying a particular passage, but when it is encountered, the Absorbed Reading surfaces. What is remarkable is that seekers still are able to continue to think they are encountering something new or something valuable.

There are passages of scripture that Contemporary Christians come to fear because of this Absorbed Reading. Contemporary Christians read these passages quickly, absently, with a nervous smile and darting eyes. They are only prevented from confronting the horror in them by not resolving the Evangelical Fallacy. If they were to fully consider the Absorbed Reading of these texts, they would be overwhelmed by the hopeless state of their souls. More so, they would be overwhelmed by the horror of the God that continually condemns them. Or—and this is the hardest route— they would have to confront the nearly subconscious itching and jerking reaction of their mind to reject the fallacy.

With this in mind, I encourage people to read on, read more. I don't discount their horror, but I try to give them a few clues to remind them that God is not a horrible beast.

Mostly, no one was paying attention. Some were looking out the window, or playing with their sugar packets. Several were looking at me, nodding like they agreed absolutely with what I was saying. I realized when I had finished and they were still looking at me and nodding, that they were veterans of these Rotary Club addresses and had perfected the art of seeming engaged while thinking about their golf game or some other thing—a kind of sleeping with their eyes open and heads nodding.

I had to clear my throat and nod at Mr. Breadesen to let him know that I was finished. He jumped up a little apologetically, feigning affability, and repeated my last words as an indication that he had followed me but with no recognition of what my words actually were.

"God is not a horrible beast. Thank you very much Pastor. Reading the Bible today. Yes, very fine, thank you. Now we will, uh, open it up for questions."

This was an unnecessary and unwelcome turn for both the good men of the Maple Lakes Rotary Club and myself. I saw several of the fellows look at their watches, more nodding from others, and my face got hot and a ringing started in my ears.

It wasn't that I had offended anyone by what I said and was afraid that I would now be called upon to defend my outrageous address. It was that no one seemed to have any inkling of what I said. No one even moved to feign that they had paid attention. It was clear that no one was going to ask a question. They were simply going to wait out the silence of the question period and then do whatever else was on the list to do. This is what made me afraid. Without thinking, I opened and shut my mouth quickly three times, and my jaw made a kind of popping sound each time. I do not know why I did this, unless it was my brain doing a systems check to see that it really had been working, that my mouth was able to open and close and make sounds, to confirm that I really had been talking previously and not just thinking.

Mr. Breadeson, following an obviously familiar routine, said, "Well we have time for just one more question." He pulled an index card from his back pocket, looked at it briefly, and asked, "Pastor, is reading the Bible important to preparing a sermon?"

I was about to give the answer that would end this for all of us. I was going to say, "Yes, it is." Then my mouth did that thing again: opened and shut quickly three times, making the popping sound. Testing, I thought. And then I said the following:

Preaching begins with reading the Bible and asking questions. Asking real questions of the Bible. Questions you don't already know the answers to. If you already know the answers, they are not real questions. You are not really reading the Bible. If you bring these fake questions into your sermon, you are just preaching the Absorbed Reading of the text. The congregation already knows the answers. This, then, is not a sermon; it is an agreement. At best a patting each other on the back. At worst very boring. A real question is not an agreement; it is an invitation. It is engaging. The people may be confused but they will not be bored.

Some verses seem to make no sense, or they seem to contain no hint of the Good News. If you find the right questions, you will find the Good News. If it scares you or bugs you or dumbfounds you, that is a real question. If you have to think about it for more than twenty minutes, that is a real question. If it makes you fall in love, believe in God, feel giddy, that is a real question. That is really reading the Bible.

If you could answer all the questions raised in the Holy Scriptures about the one true God of mercy who redeemed the world by allowing his creation to kill him and then made that very murder the means for the salvation of the world, by the time you are, say, twenty years old, or thirty, or fifty, or one hundred—then you have the wrong God.

Or the wrong questions.

Without pause this time, Mr. Breadeson repeated the last thing I said. "Or the wrong questions. Yes, the wrong questions. Thank you Pastor." He was moving toward me with his hand cocked for a handshake, but the way he was aiming it felt more like he was going to force me from the room at gunpoint. It was then that I noticed Our Senior Pastor standing by the door in the back of the Denny's Banquet and Meeting room. I froze. My mind jumped ahead and behind, trying to figure all the angles, to see what this meant. I had been right from the beginning to think there was something suspicious about this address. This was a set-up. I looked around the room for another way out. Then I saw him raise both his hands in front of his chest and push them together, palm to palm, in rapid succession. Mr. Breadeson was pumping my hand, while the rest of the Rotarians made hand movements similar to Our Senior Pastor's.

They took up a "speaker's collection" and gave me eleven dollars. I thought maybe I could use the money to buy some kerosene. The meeting broke off with one more thank-you and handshake. Our Senior Pastor came toward me, smiling. He stopped and pointed his hand the way Mr. Breadeson had. This time I knew what to do. I shook his hand and thought of things to say but didn't risk it. He said, "Have time for a quick coffee?" I nodded. I momentarily couldn't remember which direction was appropriate: up and down or back and forth, so I made kind of a circle. He took this to be assent.

"Let's get out of here and get a real cup of coffee." We got in our cars. I followed him out of the parking lot across the four-lane street into the parking lot of "The Maple: A Coffee Café and Eatery."

I looked around for familiar vehicles before I opened my car door. The time had come. I got out of the car and walked over to where he was waiting. I was ready. I had been expecting this confrontation for some time. I was sure there would be others in the Coffee Café.

From my place in the line at the counter, everything seemed normal. None of the Ministry Scouting Gatherers were there. He ordered a raspberry mocha latte. I ordered a water, then not wanting to seem suspicious, added, "Make that a flavored water."

We sat down. He started. I tightened my calves.

"I don't get much of a chance to dialogue with the team one-on-one. It seemed like we were due." I did the mouth-movement thing, testing, preparing. "Yes?" I said.

"I'm starting the visioning process for Lent and Easter, and I wanted to see the landscape from your saddle."

From my saddle, do you? I thought. I had been thinking about Lent and Easter. Obsessing really. I was thinking this would be the time to openly declare the revolution.

I had been planning to preach from Mark. I had been working on Mark for six months. It truly is a revolutionary book. It is so full of hope and the possibility of faith in its clear statements of disappointment and lack of faith. The book is so much more believable because it voices the faithlessness of Jesus' closest followers. It is precisely what the Contemporary Christians need to hear. I knew I had to be cautious in what I said about it. Obviously he was fishing.

"From my saddle?" I said.

"Yeah," he said, stabbing his straw repeatedly into the raspberry mocha and looking distracted. "Just kind of get a bearing on your path with your sermons so we can all coordinate. I have been talking to Ben, too." I think Ben is either the Chief of Worship Facilitation and Enhancement (music minister) or he is the Partner for Aesthetic Interface (the graphic artist who designs the bulletins and PowerPoint shows). "We were thinking the look and feel should be 'up'—you know, have a real kind of 'up-ness' to it. Capito? You see where we're going?"

"You're going up?" I said.

"Yes, bull's-eye! Does that fit your thinking for the sermons?"

At that moment it occurred to me that the best way to fight a revolution is to convert a general. He is not an un-smart man. He certainly has a Doctor of Ministry. Why not tell him about what I am really thinking of preaching on during Lent and Easter? Perhaps I can get through.

"How about instead of 'up' we think about 'down'?"

"Instead of 'up' . . . 'down'? Hey, talk more about that."

"It is the way Mark ends his story. You know, Mary Magdalene, and Mary the mother of James, and Salome go to the tomb to anoint the body of Jesus and find that the large stone that covered the entrance had been rolled back and Jesus was gone. They see this young man dressed in white, and he says, like, 'Don't be afraid; go tell Peter and the disciples that He will meet them in Galilee.' But get this, this is the last line in the book, 'And they went out and fled from the tomb; for trembling and astonishment had come upon them; and they said nothing to anyone, for they were afraid.'

"This is how the book ends—no resurrection, no post-resurrection appearances. The women, who had been Jesus' most faithful followers, finally fail, too. How can that be the end? This is the most un–power-and-glory Easter story there is. It is so un-up it is down and that makes up-ness possible."

Our Senior Pastor licked raspberry mocha latte foam off his lips. "The down makes the up possible, kind of a reversal thing . . . hmm."

He was thinking about it. I couldn't believe it. Maybe I had been misreading how effective I have been. This Mark stuff might just be what does it.

"You know," he said, "maybe just the 'up' without the 'down' is better. I mean I like where you are going but . . . you know what? It doesn't matter. Just do what you want. We will have enough 'up' energy. Hey, that gives me an idea. What if we package the whole Lent-Easter worshiping experience together and call it 'Re-Connection: Plugging into the Power Source of the Cross'? How does that strike you?"

"It does strike me," I said.

"OK, buddy. Thanks for the input." He got up to leave. He paused. I froze, waiting. He said, "I'm going to have to try that flavored water." He gave my shoulder a squeeze and left.

Editor's Comment

This sermon includes stage directions scrawled on the manuscript in two places. They are presumably stage directions for Lamblove by Lamblove. Although he often takes on a character and that character's point of view, in the following sermon he becomes two different characters with not only different interpretations of the text but with different levels of confidence in their interpretations.

But here's Lamblove at his best. I'm picturing this scene: The preacher walks up to the platform, walks past the pulpit placed on the stage left side, on to the band on stage right, and takes a mike from a singer's stand and moves back near the center, though still decidedly right. Placing the mike close to his mouth, head down, Phil Donahue-like, he breathes into it loudly and begins.

sermon

football coach jesus

LUKE 14:25–34

Now great multitudes accompanied him; and he turned around and faced them and said, "Unless you hate your own father and mother and wife and children and brothers and sisters, yes, even your own life, you cannot be my disciple. Unless you pick up your own cross and follow me you cannot be my disciple. Unless you renounce all that you have, you cannot be my disciple."

. . . .

Now those are pretty harsh words. Those words are hard to hear. You're thinking to yourself, "That doesn't seem like Jesus! That's not the Jesus I am used to. I thought Jesus was kind and loving and nice. I thought it was wrong to hate. It must really say something else."

So, you rub your eyes and read it again, "Unless you . . . *hate?*"

Oh, yes, it does say hate.

It doesn't seem like Jesus? It doesn't seem very nice? Well get used to it, because extreme situations call for extreme measures. And friends, this is an extreme situation.

Jesus is on his way to do a job that only one man can do. He is on his way to Jerusalem where he is going to be arrested, suffer, and die so others might live.

This is an extreme situation.

Now, that is not the end of the story. Jesus' death is not the end. Because God raised Jesus from the dead. And even though Jesus was the only one who could do *that* job, he knew, even while he was talking to that great multitude, that after his resurrection it was going to be their turn. Your turn. There was going to be a job for us to do. And he wanted to make sure we were ready.

He wanted us to prepare for the Job.

And he wanted us to know—it was not going to be easy. No, it was not always going to be nice. Because there are serious things at stake here.

The most serious thing is at stake here, and if you aren't prepared to go all the way, don't even start the trip.

Let's read the book. Jesus goes on to tell a couple of stories to make the point, he says:

Which of you, if you're going to build a tower, doesn't first sit down and count the cost to see if you have enough money to complete the job? Otherwise, you've laid the foundation and you're not able to finish what you started.

Get this: then he goes on to say:

All those who saw that unfinished tower began to mock that builder, saying, "This man began to build and was not able to finish. What king going into battle will not first sit down and figure out whether he is able with ten thousand to win that battle against twenty thousand? And if he figures he is not he sends out his ambassador and asks for terms of peace." So, therefore, whoever of you does not renounce all that you have you cannot be my disciple.

This is an extreme situation, and it calls for extreme disciples.

Jesus wants to make sure we understand. Not because he is being mean. Come on, Jesus is doing this out of love—love for us, because he wants us to understand what it is going to take. Extreme situations call for extreme love—tough love.

And this is indeed an extreme situation. Not just the situation in Jesus' time, but today. *We* are in an extreme situation.

There are things at stake; the whole game is at stake. It's like Jesus is a football coach in the locker room at half time. It's a close game and it's now or never. Coach Jesus is getting his team up for the second half. He is talking, not just to that great multitude but to all of us on his team. He's saying:

What's it going to take to win this one? It's going to take everything you have. Your family, your mother and father, your kids, everything. This is job one. Are you willing to give it all? Well, decide now.

Count the cost. *El Quanto Costus* in the original Latin. Which literally means "count the cost."

Are you going to be able to finish the game? Because if you can't, don't even start. Because if you can't, what is going to happen? People will mock you, laugh at you, and make fun of you.

If you tell people you are a disciple of Jesus, and you can't go all the way, you know what you'll be? An extreme loser.

So, decide now.

Jesus says out of love—oh yes, and it is *tough love*—decide now because if you can't go all the way it gets worse than having people laugh at you.

Verse 34 says: Salt is good; but if salt has lost its taste, how shall its saltiness be restored? How shall it be restored?

Ask any scientist and he'll tell you: once sodium has lost its saltiness, it is a *fact* of chemistry that it is impossible for it to be restored. Jesus goes on, "Then that salt is fit neither for the land nor the dung heap."

There is a phrase I like: Souled Out.

You know what that means? Souled Out. It means that you have given everything, sold everything to follow Jesus. It means that you have given all that you have, your entire soul—not just part of it, not three quarters of it, but your entire soul—to follow Jesus. It means you're an extreme disciple. It means you're going to finish the job. Jesus says going all the way is the only way to be my disciple.

Let's be extreme disciples—let's get out there—we have a job to do!

The Preacher puts the mike back in the stand and walks back across the platform, slows at the communion table as if going to take communion at the end of the sermon. He then moves on to the pulpit on the left side of the stage, arranges his notes on the pulpit, takes a minute—deflates—and begins, a different character now.

. . . .

[*speaking with almost a hiss*] Man, I would like to kill that Jesus. I would like to kill that football coach Jesus. I would like to kill that football coach God. I would like to kill that football coach preacher.

But it is very hard. They live inside of me. Even now when I read the Bible, the first voice I hear is that football coach preacher and his football coach Jesus. After hearing that all my life, after hearing those sermons and interpretation of the texts by so many different teachers and preachers, after using them myself so many times, it is very hard to kill them off.

But they have to die.

They have to be gotten rid of, if I ever want to figure this stuff out—if I ever want to know how to follow Jesus.

That football coach Jesus is just too easy—too easy to believe and too easy to dismiss.

It's too easy to believe because it echoes the culture I was raised in, that I live in: Finish what you started. If you're going to do something, do it right. Try harder. You can do anything if you just try hard enough. And if you don't accomplish the things you want to, you didn't try hard enough. Jesus wants you to try harder; Jesus wants you to pull yourself up by your own bootstrap.

This Jesus never considers the fact that you might not even have any boots. Never takes into account that you might be trying really, really hard and still not be able to make it.

What if I count the cost and I really, really believe I have what it takes? I really am willing to give everything, to go all the way, but then along the way I find out I don't. I don't give everything; I take something back. I screw up. I lose my saltiness and there is no way to get it back. How shall it be restored? It's dung-heap time; I get slaughtered by the opposing army; I am laughed at for not being able to finish the job.

Football coach Jesus is this weird mix of a motivational speaker and a mean dad shaming me for being lazy. *You have to go all the way, give up everything, finish what you started.* Mean-dad-football-coach-Jesus makes me want to cry and give up.

It is too easy to believe because it echoes the culture I live in.

But it is also too easy to dismiss. Jesus wants me to hate my mom and dad? Well, *there's* a good reason not to believe in Jesus.

All I have to do is use my brain to figure out that the football coach sermon is ridiculous. If I can imagine a God who is more loving and intelligent than the one I find in the Bible, then it is obviously time to get a new God.

Such a flat and unforgiving God is too easy, and it is a lie. You mix a little truth with lies, and you put them in the mouth of a competent public speaker, and you say it over and over again, and you guarantee that there will always be enough work for the therapists.

Now, you know what is hard? What is hard is to actually use my brain and passion (my soul?) and try to figure out what this really says. Because I can't believe it the way he says it [*gesturing to the point where football coach preacher was standing*], and I desperately do not want to dismiss it, because I believe there is Good News and I believe it can be found in our sacred texts.

So I rub my eyes and I read it again. Not with the sense that hard work and perseverance will elicit the meaning that I want. Not simply to explain away my own horror. But I give myself to it completely with trust that it is the book of the God that knows me and loves me. It is the book that our people have found this great Good News in for thousands of years.

And I try to remind myself that this text is not about me. It is about Jesus.

I try to remember that every word of judgment is not about eternal life in hell but is simply a word of judgment, and wrong actions are judged all the time.

I do have to continually fight off football coach Jesus, but it is the good fight.

Luke tells a story about Jesus on the way to Jerusalem with his disciples—a broad term used to describe anyone who chose to follow him—his Twelve Apostles, Pharisees, the curious, the outsiders, and the unclean. The story is framed beautifully: everything from chapter 9 to chapter 19 takes place as they travel to Jerusalem. Luke repeats *on the way* and *the way* to emphasize that Jesus is teaching his followers what it means to follow in the way, to "go with" Jesus.

In the beginning of chapter 14, it is the Sabbath, and as he does many times, Jesus attends the synagogue in the town he is passing through on his way to Jerusalem. He is invited to the synagogue leader's house for a meal afterward, and some of his disciples, Pharisees among them, come with him.

Only Pharisees can eat with other Pharisees because they are a sect dedicated to ritual purity. In their understanding, one maintains a right relationship with God by remaining pure, and one remains pure by keeping company only with others who are pure. In Mediterranean culture at the time, strict rules divide people. One's place in society is defined by those with whom one associates. The primary unit is the extended family, and it is seen as a whole. If a member achieves greatness, the family achieves greatness. If one of them is humiliated, all of them are humiliated.

Meals are the clearest reflection of your associations: you are who you eat with. Further, mealtime politics define one's relative position within the group. The closer you sit to the host, the greater your position of honor.

Jesus teaches at the meal, which is the custom in these situations. First he tells a story about how one should take the position of least honor at a meal. Then he tells a story about how a great meal was given and none of the right people (the pure association) came. Instead, the host went out and invited all the impure people (everyone from all the lower classes and all the foreigners), and he ate with them.

Jesus is teaching his disciples what it means to follow the way of the new kingdom, which reorders society from one of exclusion to one of inclusion. The *way* is about continually widening the circle.

After the meal, he leaves and his disciples follow him. And he turns to them and says, "Unless you hate your own father and mother and wife and children and brothers and sisters, yes, even your own life, you cannot be my disciple."

Now after all that explanation, these words do not sound less harsh, less hard to hear. In fact, they are even more extreme. Because they are not simply talking about having a bad relationship with your family; they are about abandoning the foundation of the culture. Jesus says you will have to give up the associations that define who you are. And you will have to count the cost. He is saying that if you follow me, according to the old calculus, you will bring disgrace and dishonor to your family because you will be on the way with the impure, the lower classes, even foreigners. You will give up your family to be with one who will be executed as a criminal and a traitor. In the end, you have to be willing to give up your own life, because there is a very real chance that if they kill me they will kill you, too.

This is much more than hating your family. This is transforming the culture you were raised in, that you live in. He wants them to know what it really means to go with him on the way.

Now here is the beauty of Luke's structure: It starts with Jesus being followed by Pharisees. In the middle, disciples are following him, and he tells them what that will mean for them. Now at the end, they are following him and who joins the group? In chapter 15, verses 1 and 2: their mothers and fathers and brothers and sisters don't join them; other Pharisees don't join them, but tax collectors and sinners join them. This is exactly the situation that Jesus explained to them. Here is what the reoriented world, the Kingdom of God, looks like. They have to count the cost and determine if they can go this far, if they can be on the way with the other, the impure.

And they say, "Look at this, he receives sinners and eats with them."

Well, yes, of course he does. And he receives you and eats with you, too, and in the New Kingdom, you will all eat together. That is the point of chapter 14.

But they are not ready to go this far yet. So what does Jesus do? He keeps teaching them, through the next couple of chapters. Same lesson, different approach.

Now it gets harder. What does this all mean? How am I supposed to follow Jesus?

I know that it is not about the old calculus of the football coach Jesus who defines a right relationship with God as being pure, who defines purity and impurity by my ability to go all the way and never screw up. That is contrary to the text.

If the new calculus is about reorienting my world, what does that mean? What is the foundation of my culture that needs to be upended? And how is that accomplished by following this God whose journey ends in death at the hands of the ones God loves?

Editor's Comment
....

In this entry, Lamblove's struggle to do his job every day seems to be more about his own mental state than his professed struggle to work within the institutions of the conspiracy. At some points in his writings, he seems to be a genuine misanthrope. His professed revolution seems to be aimed at freeing people who actually irritate him quite a lot.

journal entry
(the parking lot is
a dangerous place)

I have had so many conversations with people while hanging on to the driver's side door of my car. I stand there clutching, with one leg stuck inside up to my thigh and my body twisted to face the instigator with my car door between us like a shield or the confessional screen. Which one is it?

Why so many conversations in this position? What is it about? Protection? Transition?

I am willing to accept that it is likely the only place people can catch me (I do feel caught). The parking lot is a dangerous place.

Weekdays when I arrive at work, I look over the acres of parking lot between me and the doors of the Ministry Center and wonder if I can make it across the expanse without being stopped to chat or share or to be "care-fronted."

It is a long way, the parking lot is monstrous, and all the pastors have assigned spots at the very back of the lot as a symbol of our willingness to put others first. On Sundays, those with a Community Commitment are directed to the middle sides of the lot; the Invested Seekers to the middle center; Investigators and First Time Visitors park front center. It really is a disincentive to commit if parking is a personal priority. If I ever need extra money, I will write a book called "The Theology of the Parking Lot." It will sell, provided it doesn't contain any theology, but there are probably already a dozen like it on the shelf. There might even be a Parking Ministries section in the Heaven's Borders Bookstore and Café.

My real fear, as I measure the distance to the door, is that the emotional weight of knowing what lies inside the Ministry Center will become too much for me to support with my weak coffee-and-toast-fed body. (Oh, I do eat an apple sometimes.)

Once inside the doors, I catch my breath and do some calming visualization exercises to help me make it through the fluorescent-lit, incandescent-accented oppression to my office.

I have a crazy fear of the public space inside. I feel safe in my office and safe in the pulpit but dread the hallways and atrium, the mezzanine, gathering commons, lounge areas, and even the classrooms. I am particularly afraid of the classrooms.

I have only taught one class. It was a disaster. I was supposed to teach the "Inquiring Minds" section of the Adults Interactive Curriculum, which is designed to move Investigators to Invested Seeker status. I didn't want to use the workbook I was given, so they said they could find a study guide. I said I wanted to use the Bible, but they said that the Bible doesn't come in until Adults Online, in year two, when Invested Seekers move to Community Commitment. I said, "Oh."

I don't remember the class, except the struggle to be Interactive while fending off full-scale panic attacks (that's when I learned the calming visualization exercises). That and the Vice President for Explorer Growth telling me that as a result of my class, almost thirty people had to be downgraded to Interested Wanderers—a growth category, he told me pointedly, which they had not used since 1993. I was removed from the Senior Explorer Guide roster.

Before they built the staff dining room—Navigator's Galley, Partners Pantry (I don't know what they call it now)—they held the monthly Mapping Luncheon in one of the large classrooms. After one particularly intense panic attack, I stopped going. When the Vice President for Guide Support and Growth (the staff police, if you ask me) stopped me in the Connection Commons and said in that very nonconfrontational way (which is very confrontational), "*Hey,* Buddy." Watch out when they call you Buddy. If it is combined with the hand-to-the-shoulder move, run. "We've missed you at the Mapping Luncheons lately. Everything on target?"

I told him I didn't go because I was afraid of the classrooms. He said, with a half smile (trying to decide if this particular "off target Guide" needed concerned understanding or playful banter, and showed the indecision with his mouth). "Afraid?"

I said, "Yeah, I'm afraid to go in them; they terrify me." I could see through his eyes into his head. He was searching his hard drive for the appropriate response. Unable to find a match, he offered, "Well, keep your compass in front of you."

"I will," I said.

When they moved the monthly Luncheons to the Partners Pantry, I still stayed away and no one said anything.

I am rambling. What I was getting at was this:

Sunday, after the fifth service, I thought I had waited long enough. I checked out the parking lot from the window of the media center. Only about fifty cars were left, and no one seemed to be hovering around my car, or in striking distance. So I put my bag over my shoulder and went for it, through the administration atrium, out the doors, past the valet kiosk, and into the expanse. I walked determinedly and tried to look preoccupied, late for something. I have promised myself I won't run. Even I understand the emotional ill-health it would display to be seen daily fleeing from one's workplace. I make it to my car, chastise myself for being such a freak, unlock the door (by actually putting the key in the lock. Certainly mine is the only car in the lot that doesn't chirp as I approach it), open it, and, as I just put one leg in, I hear, "*Hey,* Buddy." I twist my body, grasp the car door—now I am certain, it is a shield—and begin the conversation.

It was a "just saying hi" conversation that ranged freely from stock portfolios and awesome new movies to harmless gossip and how pumped the spirit was in the third and fourth service compared to the first, second, and fifth. Now finally to come back to my point. As he said, "pumped the spirit was," I thought, I have so many conversations in this position that I might be damaging my right hip socket.

I should just take my leg out of the car and turn to face my conversation buddy with my whole body. But I fear that gesture might lengthen the conversation by as much as twelve minutes.

It was then that I felt a wave of euphoria, originating from my right hip socket, bearing on its crest this simple thought: quit your job. Why risk the physical impairment? Why risk the madness? Why in the world would I be complicit in the conspiracy? I could just quit. Not abandon the revolution but attack from outside.

I said the appropriate words and made the appropriate body movements that accompany the end of a casual conversation. Although at an inappropriate time—he was, I think, in the middle of a sentence—and drove home feeling free, giddy, singing to myself, "hey buddy, hey buddy, hey buddy, I quit."

Now, back home, I seemed to have left the freedom in the car. It is not at all clear that I should quit.

I always assumed that they would fire me. I was looking over past journal entries. I wrote at one point, "I am going to stop being afraid to say what I want to say. What do I have to lose? I can't launch a revolution while worrying if I am going to make people feel bad. What is the worst that can happen? They fire me—I would love that. I want them to fire me. I can't quit. That would be the worst kind of sin. That would be saying, these people didn't matter, were not worth loving. It would be to abandon them. But if I am fired, I am free."

So, I can't quit. But I can speak more plainly. I could preach a sermon that *would* get me fired.

I will prepare a sermon that names the Contemporary Christian Culture Conspiracy, but I will give it a name like, "Faith at Work: Working with Your Faith, *At Work!*" That way they might not be on guard. They might not put the sound-canceling device on. I can enlist Amy. I'll ask her to sit in the back at the beginning of the sermon and then move up to the front half way through, close enough so she could hear my voice, even without amplification. Then she will be able to tell whether or not the device is on. The device can't work on an unamplified voice. Can it? Could they silence my words even before they come out of my mouth?

Editor's Comment

. . . .

Although many of the sermons using a preacher
character serve as critiques of contemporary
christian culture preachers, other preacher-
character sermons seem to be Lamblove examining his
own role as a preacher, sometimes simultaneously boldly
proclaiming his revolutionary message and questioning
the legitimacy of his right to proclaim anything
to anyone. Lamblove is not only interested in the
role of the preacher in the conspiracy and
the church, but (and maybe primarily) his own role
as preacher. I wonder if his whole revolution is
subconsciously his attempt to deal with his failure
as a preacher. Why in this sermon, which he claimed
would name the conspiracy, does he back off at
the end, turning it on himself?

sermon

penlight jesus

LUKE 4:14–30

And he came to Nazareth, where he had been brought up; and he went to the synagogue, as his custom was, on the Sabbath day. And he stood up to read; and there was given to him the book of the prophet Isaiah. He opened the book and found the place where it was written,

"The Spirit of the Lord is upon me, because he has anointed me to preach good news to the poor. He has sent me to proclaim release to the captives and recovery of sight to the blind, to set free the oppressed, to proclaim the acceptable year of the Lord."

And he closed the book, and gave it back to the attendant, and sat down; and the eyes of all in the synagogue were fixed on him. And he began to say to them, "Today this scripture has been fulfilled in your hearing." And all spoke well of him, and wondered at the gracious words which proceeded out of his mouth; and they said, "Is not this Joseph's son?" and he said to them, "Doubtless you will quote to me this proverb, 'Physician, heal yourself; what we have heard you did at Capernaum, do here also in your own country.'" And he said, "Truly, I say to you, no prophet is acceptable in his own country. But in truth, I tell you, there were many widows in Israel in the days of Elijah, when the heaven was shut up three years and six months, when there came a great famine over all the land; and Elijah was sent to none of them but only to Zarephath, in the land of Sidon, to a woman who was a widow. And there were many lepers in Israel in the time of the prophet Elisha; and none of them was cleansed, but only Naman the Syrian." When they heard this, all in the synagogue were filled with wrath. And they rose up and put him out of the city, and led him to the brow of the hill on which their city was built, that they might throw him down headlong. But passing through the midst of them he went away.

. . . .

I have this recurring nightmare that I think I've told you about before. I go to sleep and I wake up in this future world that is controlled by a Contemporary Christian Culture Conspiracy.

All that is wrong with the way we practice Christian faith in our present world comes to the surface in this End Times Contemporary Christian Culture government that rules the world. It is everything that is bad about Christianity mixed up with capitalism and self-help psychology, and it's all put together in a regime that controls everything. It's sort of like a fascist state but everyone says they're really glad to see you.

In my dream I feel so helpless and I am always alone: everyone else is part of the conspiracy, this ruling Contemporary Christian Culture. It is everywhere, and it doesn't look like any kind of Christianity that I've ever known. It is no longer about the Good News. It is bad news. It is all about marketing and personal satisfaction, and I am always so helpless and alone. There is nothing I can do; nobody else gets it but me. Nobody can see the Conspiracy because they are all part of it. I want to say, Go back and read the book. I want to scream as loud as I can, *Wake up! Look what you've done!*

I have this dream almost every night and it is always the same. Until last Tuesday.

Last Tuesday in my nightmare something different happened. I find myself backstage (in that dreamlike way where you somehow know where you are) in a convention hall during the world-wide convocation of the Contemporary-Christian-Culture-Government-Ruling-Convention thing. I am back there and I realize they have mistaken me for the keynote preacher. And

I realize—now is my chance. So I sit down and quickly I start to scribble. I take all my hopelessness and desire and anger, and I gather up my best fire and brimstone, and I try to put it in a sermon. And then a guy comes to get me. He shakes my hand and says he's really glad to see me. He leads me out onto the stage and to the pulpit. I put my scribbled sermon down, and I look at them and I say in a bellowing, confident, preacher's voice:

This is the Good News.

Jesus stands up in the synagogue and reads from the scroll of Isaiah, "The Spirit of the Lord is upon me, because he has anointed me to bring good news to the poor. He has sent me to proclaim release to the captives and recovery of sight to the blind, to let the oppressed go free, to proclaim the year of the Lord's favor."

And then I stare them down, and I say:

This is not about you. This, in Luke's story about Jesus, is God's mission statement. It is a restatement of God's long-held purpose for interacting with the world. This is the decisive reiteration of God's purpose because it is spoken by God's incarnation. And it is not about you.

This is not about you on your knees at the altar claiming a personal Lord and savior. This is about those people who are brought to their knees because their legs have given out, because the weight of depression and hopelessness have drained them of the ability to get up.

This is about the whole city you live in, the whole world. This is a community thing. Salvation has nothing to do with eternal self-interest. Salvation has nothing to do with building your own security pod that will jettison you to heaven when the world gets too hateful or your body gives out.

Salvation is about reconciling the profound separation of God's people into individuals that results in turning individuals into strangers and strangers into enemies. Salvation is about the reintegration of the isolated into the community. Salvation is about freeing those who are made captive by systems of injustice that keep down their ability to make a living wage while simultaneously twisting their minds to desire material markers of so-called freedom they can only possess through self-destruction.

This passage in Luke is the decisive reiteration of God's purpose in the world, spoken by the incarnation of God. And it is not about you. It is about something God is doing. And God will continue doing it whether you are a part of it or not. God's plan for the reorientation of the world does not depend on your personal decision.

The personalization of salvation—the individualization of Christianity—is not the result of honest interpretation of our holy scriptures, faithful adherence to our tradition, clear application of our reason, or divine revelation from the spirit of God.

The personalization of salvation is the result of the twisting of all these things, the misinterpretation of a selection of scriptural passages taken out of context. Chief among them is John 3:16. This is the text that your Contemporary Christian Culture has held up as the Mission Statement of God. Do you know it by heart? Do you know it in the King James version? "For God so loved the world that he sent his only son, that whosoever believeth in him should not perish but have everlasting life."

This text has been ripped from the story it is in, and these words of Jesus have been fashioned into a club to beat individuals to their knees to accept their personal Lord and savior. It is presented, time and time again, surrounded by so much garbage of personal piety and manipulation that it always comes out sounding like Jesus is making individual trips from heaven to knock on the door of some poor Sunday school student's heart to see if he can get in.

This weak, robe-wearing, door-knocking Jesus, who would be thwarted by the indecision of a twelve-year-old, is no savior. That is not at all what the story is about. Read the whole thing. At least read what comes before it. "And just as Moses lifted up the serpent in the wilderness, so must the Son of Man be lifted up, that who ever believes in him may have eternal life" (John 3:14–15).

"As Moses lifted up the serpent in the wilderness . . ." This is not about individual salvation. This is a reference to God's redemption of the People of Israel, God's chosen people. Moses didn't go around from person to person, asking them to look into their hearts.

And to make it perfectly clear, look at what comes after it: "Indeed, God did not send his son into the world to condemn the world, but in order that the world might be saved" (John 3:17–21). The world. God's plan is not about you. It is about the whole world.

Verse 19 reads: "This is the judgment, that the light has come into the world, and people loved the darkness rather than the light because their deeds were evil." The light has come into the world and exposed the evil we practice. This is a blinding, all-encompassing light; this is not a little flashlight that Jesus brings with him when he gets into your heart and shines around in the darkness inside you to see if you have any evil tucked away in the nooks and crannies of your soul. No, this is a worldwide light of Justice exposing the atrocities and evil we have come to accept as normal.

Who is this personal penlight Jesus? He's no savior. God's Son came to reorient the whole world.

Back up even further to the beginning of Luke 4 and the story of the temptation of Jesus. In the final temptation, the devil uses holy scripture to tempt Jesus to save himself. This is what happens right before Jesus proclaims God's purpose for him: "The Spirit of the Lord is upon me, because he has anointed me to bring good news to the poor. He has sent me to proclaim release to the captives and recovery of sight to the blind, to let the oppressed go free, to proclaim the year of the Lord's favor" (Luke 4:18–19).

The devil uses scripture to tempt him to make God's purpose his own salvation. Is that any different from some Sunday school teacher or evangelist using John 3:16 to manipulate us into doing the same thing? Luke's placement of these two scriptures can only be there to invite comparison.

Jesus stands up in the synagogue in Nazareth and proclaims God's purpose for himself and for the world. And God's purpose is not about you; it is about the poor, the captives, the blind, the oppressed, the depressed, the isolated, and the hopeless.

You want to memorize something? Memorize that. Luke 4:18 and 19. Put that on a T-shirt. Put that on a sign and hold that up at football games.

After Jesus reads this proclamation of God's purpose, he sits down and says, "This scripture has been fulfilled today. I am that anointed one God has sent." All the people of his hometown forget about the content of that scripture and only hear that Jesus, the son of

Joseph, one of their own, is the Savoir God has sent and immediately move to turn the situation to their own self-interest.

They say, "Doctor, cure yourself, cure your own. If you, the promised savior, are one of our own, then do for us all those miracles and things we've heard about you doing for other people. After all, if you would do great works for strangers, what even more amazing things will you do for your own people?"

And Jesus responds, "I'm not here to heal the healthy, but the sick. Do you remember the story when there was a great drought, and there was severe famine over the land and there were many hungry widows here in Israel? Elijah wasn't sent to them but to Zarephath a gentile widow in Sidon, some distance away. And remember the story of the prophet Elisha? There were many lepers in Israel and none of them were cleansed except Naaman, who was the leader of our enemy's armies." Sound familiar? ("This is not about you.")

When all Jesus' hometown friends heard this, they were filled with rage and they grabbed him and tried to throw him off a cliff. What is the appropriate response?

The appropriate response when God's purpose is proclaimed is not to ask, "What is in it for me?" but "How can I help?" and to join with God's purpose. The rest of the book of Luke is filled with examples of the appropriate responses. The remaining chapters are an invitation to join Jesus in carrying out God's purpose to bring release, restoration, recovery, and freedom—a complete reorientation—to the world.

The personalization of salvation and the individualization of Christianity are not the result of honest interpretation of our holy scriptures, faithful adherence to our tradition, clear application of our reason, or divine rev-elation from the spirit of God. They are the result of giving in to the temptation of the devil to save yourself.

This is not about you. This is about what God is doing.

After all, what takes more faith—to believe that God can save you and offer personal fulfillment and comfort, or to believe that God can reorient the whole world from one of hate, greed, fear and personal gain, to one ruled by peace and justice? A world where there is Good News for the poor, release for the captives, the recovery of sight for the blind—where the oppressed are free, and all live according to God's good favor. What takes more faith—to believe that God can save you or that God is going to save the whole world and wants you to help?

So, that was my big finish line. I looked out there just to see if they all got it, if I had pierced them. And you know how dreams are, as I look out there, it is no longer the convention of this evil worldwide Contemporary Christian Culture Conspiracy. I see these banners and I realize it is a surprise party for my birthday. Everybody that I know and care about is there. I can see my mom and dad and my friends and my grandma. My grandma is the one who helped me memorize John 3:16. I look out there and I see that, sitting there, in the third row back, is me, and the "me" sitting there has this stunned, confused look on his face. And then my grandma stands up and she looks at the me sitting in the audience and she looks at the me standing on the stage and she says, "Surprise."

Editor's Comment

At this point I feel I should refine my characteri-
zation of Lamblove as "crazy." From "Penlight Jesus"
it seems that he has taken his notion of a contemporary Christian culture conspiracy out of the
pages of his journal and pronounced them from
the pulpit. I am not a licensed psychologist or any
kind of mental health professional and am therefore
unable to make any responsible actual diagnosis. Even
if I were a mental health professional, it would still
be irresponsible for me to make a diagnosis of the
Reverend based solely on this collection of writings
from a very limited period of his life—not to mention
their questionable (if not unknown) origin. I have,
however, called him crazy, and at times I have felt
that that was not completely fair. At one point
I seriously considered omitting the term from the
prelude but could not bring myself to part with the
phrase unknown-crazy-revolutionary-preacher. I just
liked the idea; it amused me.

I have wondered if his talk of the conspiracy
and his post-apocalyptic visions were just kind of
made up, if they were a convention he used to talk
about the state of the church or of his life. They
might have started out that way, but it seems that
he has come to a point where he believes them or
they seem real to him. And this scares him, or he
is worried that it doesn't scare him. I don't think
I am assuming the role of a psychologist or over-
reaching my role as editor/biographer to say that
Lamblove has become paranoid and delusional. His claim
of apocalyptic visions, his talk of a contemporary

Christian culture conspiracy and his suspicions of a secret sound-canceling device seem, even to a layman, to be the marks of someone who is, in a clinical sense, unhinged. I don't know if unhinged is an actual clinical diagnosis. A mental health professional would know.

journal entry
(Amy Knows something)

When I turned in my information for the worship folder on Thursday, I hoped Amy was in the office. I would be able to speak to her relatively discreetly but felt it wasn't wise to speak too openly. It might be risky to try and find out exactly what she knows about the conspiracy, but I will be able to confirm that she knows something and, if she is willing, elicit her help in the fight.

"Rubber to the road," I said. She responded with the same words, reflecting my general greeting to everyone in the office. (She was the only one. Several other Support Team Members looked at me suspiciously—with irritation?—no, suspiciously.) I gave my sermon title and scripture text information to the Support Team Member for Data Entry and lingered by the mailbox, pretending to pick up my mail. This was made somewhat difficult by the fact that my mail cubby was obviously empty.

Amy picked up my cue. She came over and said, "I throw out the junk mail for you, since you don't come by that often."

I looked in the box again and then looked at her and then couldn't find what I was going to say. She kind of smiled with the left half of her mouth and said, "I leave everything else in there."

Smile. I should smile too. With the right side of my mouth? I tried. It was a grimace. "Thank you," I told her. I looked at her. She looked at me, tilted her head slightly to the right and smiled bigger. She has some code worked out. I tilted my head slightly to the left and tried to smile, managing better this time, at the last minute decided to show teeth and then deciding against it. She laughed. I had apparently figured out the code and responded correctly. She might not understand the complexity of the conspiracy, but Amy knows something and she was ready to help.

"Could you do me one more favor, Amy?"

"Of course," she said.

"Could you sit in the front this Sunday, the very front, while I am preaching?" I spoke casually, trying to be careful not to say anything that anyone who might be listening could pick up on. "You could start out in the back and then move to the front. That way," I paused and tried to emphasize this part using her code: I jutted the top of my head forward. "You could see if you can hear me."

She jutted her head forward and said, "It would be my pleasure."

About five minutes into the sermon, she came down a side aisle and sat in the front row. Right before the end of the sermon I looked down at her. She mouthed the words, "I—can—hear—you."

Amy knows something.

Editor's Comment

....

The following note, which I have excerpted, was paper-clipped to the sermon that follows it. From the type of paper and the torn edge, it is obvious that it was ripped from the journal. Lamblove did not want this sermon to be read without this journal entry. This is the only case where Lamblove has so pointedly insisted on providing a context for a sermon. He says he was invited to preach at a new church started by the mother church that employed him. He was asked to preach on prayer and was given the Lord's Prayer in Luke as his text. He chose instead the verses that come after the Lord's Prayer.

He writes, "I wanted them to understand how hard it is to pray, 'Our Father,' to understand the horror and the risk involved." This of course might be true, but with Lamblove it might not. I cannot help wondering if this sermon is autobiographical. The preacher-father figure he uses again raises the question of why he has so many sermons about preachers.

I have conjectured before that this was a way for him to highlight the role of the preacher in the contemporary Christian culture conspiracy and the revolution's dependence on bringing them down. Further, I have surmised that he might be using the preacher characters to examine his own role as a preacher. I now have to posit the possibility that it is not his own role as preacher that he is trying to come to grips with but that of his real-life father that haunts him. This kind of wound he exposes in the sermon, "Preacher and a Drunk," could explain his sense of displacement in the world and certainly in the culture of the church. This is, I know, the most hackneyed armchair psychology, but hey, I really don't have a lot to work with here.

Of course it could be, as Lamblove claims, a device to illustrate his main point. I have no idea if his father was a preacher. But why paper-clip the journal entry to the sermon? With that gesture he seems to be saying, "I want you to know this is absolutely not about my father." Part of me thinks he doth protest too much. On the other hand, I don't want to ascribe such a father to him based on such little evidence. Either way, it is a pretty dark sermon.

First, the journal entry.

journal entry
(Generation Jesus)

Last Sunday evening I found myself sitting in the Charles Coleson Jr. High Gymnasium. I was asked to preach in this new church plant. (They call new churches "plants" because the mother church has seeded them.) Our Senior Pastor says we must seed one a year. In my understanding of physiology it is the father who spills the seed, but all involved use the "mother church" metaphor, probably to avoid the unpleasant yet more accurate image of Our Senior Pastor's continued desire to find fertile soil for his genetic material. The gym is completely unadorned except for the scoreboard, the basketball hoops, a sagging "Go Panthers" banner at one end, and a sagging "Generation Jesus" banner at the other. The latter hangs above a band that is set up on the gym floor, with a Plexiglas lectern in front.

I went the week before I was to preach to scope out the situation, to see who I would be preaching to and to gauge the level of anxiety the situation would cause me, which I discovered was great. I sat on a metal folding chair surrounded by people who look just like me, dress like me, and consume like me, listening to some ill-conceived hybrid of post-pop/punk/pre-emo praise song, which ends up sounding like any other praise song—three lines of bad poetry repeated endlessly to the inane strum of a guitar. This is just a little more whiney and the guitar happens to be plugged in.

The sign outside said, "Contemporary and Alternative Worship Service Here!" and I could not help wondering what this might actually be an alternative to. What tradition was it that became so tired or oppressive or corrupt or irrelevant, so excruciatingly painful to participate in, that *this* was the preferred alternative? Or is it just that the tradition is old (so old, you know, like old people) and my peers wanted something contemporary?

While I was lost in thought, the post-pop/punk/pre-emo praise band had given way to an energetic young hipster talking. He was going on and on about how he was not really a "Preacher" like some old, bad "Preacher" (and he kept doing that annoying thing with his fingers), but he liked to think of himself as a "Faith-Sharer" and he was not going to "preach" at us like some old, bad person who "preaches" at people but was going to do a little "faith-sharing." I tuned him out again and started writing ideas for my sermon on a flyer listing future Generation Jesus events.

They wanted me to talk about prayer. Now I know why they kept saying the word "talk" and not "preach." I don't know how to talk. I barely know how to pray. I just kept thinking how dark it all seemed. How dark the scene made me feel. How it seemed impossible for the light of the Good News to break through this embryonic Contemporary Christian Culture Church. You can already see in the Faith-Sharer's eyes the certainty that it will one day grow up to be a Worship Center. It felt necessary for me to point out the darkness. The Conspiracy can only be stopped by seeing the darkness. Only then can one see the light. This seems essential for the revolution. Not only to use my sermon weapon against the most egregious monster churches of the conspiracy but to slay their children before they are allowed to grow. And these infant Conspiracy Churches are being birthed everywhere. Not only does Our Senior Pastor seed one a year, but hundreds more like him are impregnating community centers, movie theaters, warehouse spaces, and high school auditoriums all over the county.

I knew I would need a very serious weapon.

sermon

preacher and a drunk

LUKE 11:9–13

So I say to you, ask, and it will be given you; search and you will find; knock, and the door will be opened for you. For everyone who asks receives, and everyone who searches finds, and for everyone who knocks, the door will be opened. Is there anyone among you who, if your child asks for a fish, will give a snake instead of a fish? OR if the child asks for an egg, will give a scorpion? If you then, who are evil, know how to give good gifts to your children, how much more will the heavenly Father give the Holy Spirit to those who ask him!

. . . .

Sometimes I have to talk about the darkness to separate it from the light.

My dad was a preacher and a drunk. And from the time I was five until the time I was fifteen he was a radio evangelist. I know it seems funny. Just the notion of a radio evangelist is funny, maybe even ridiculous. No one actually knows a radio evangelist (or the son of a radio evangelist), but it was a job that suited him perfectly. It allowed him, in a way that no other job would, to be both a preacher and a drunk.

He couldn't stand in the pulpit with a glass of Old Granddad, but he could sit behind the microphone with one.

I used to listen to him at home, lying in bed, thinking I could hear him refill his glass. He would be saying something or talking to a caller or praying, and I felt sure I could hear a pouring sound, a glass being filled up, the gurgle or a burp of the whiskey coming out of the bottle. Sometimes I know I heard the lip of the bottle knock into the rim of the glass. Faint in the background—a little whoosh, gurgle, clink. Whoosh, gurgle, clink.

Sometimes I would try to count how many refills he would have, and then I would add a few, being sure I'd missed some, or guessing that he refilled on the breaks.

We lived in the California desert about a hundred miles east of San Diego, seventy-five miles south of Palm Springs, fifty miles west of Yuma, Arizona, and fifteen miles north of the Mexican border. My dad had a church there in Plaster City when I was born. They mined gypsum there. That's why they called it Plaster City. Four years after I was born, the mine went dry (or tapped out—I don't know what mines do, whatever, it was empty I guess).

Pretty much everybody moved away. And that meant his congregation. That's when he became a radio evangelist—he had already been working on the drunk part for a while, as far as I knew.

I don't know the particulars of how he got started, or how it worked technically, but he converted the nursery of the church into a broadcast booth, and his show was transmitted over this high-powered AM station just across the border in Mexico. You could pick it up from California to Texas and all the way up to Utah. His show was from ten at night until two in the morning. Again, perfect hours for his dual occupation.

I don't think it occurred to me until much later than it should have that being a preacher and a drunk were somehow inconsistent. You know how it is when you're a kid; things just are the way they are.

The problems with having an alcoholic as a dad are many, but they say, and I agree completely, that the most damaging are the unpredictable behaviors. Lack of structure denies a kid the chance to ever really get any kind of footing in the world. It never allows for laying down any foundations for a kid to build a life on. You never knew what the rules were or what was expected of you.

One night after supper I might be scrambling around, gathering everything up to take out the garbage, and he would say, "Quit your rushing around, don't worry about it. You can do that in the morning." And the next week after supper I'd think, I'll just do it in the morning. Then I'd go to do my homework, only to have him come smashing into my room with the kitchen garbage pail yelling and screaming about how lazy and worthless I was; then I'd get beat with that garbage pail.

I always said, my dad had really strict rules; I just never knew what they were.

His show was called, "The Daily Bread with Pastor Bruce." The format was pretty standard. He would open with the Bible reading of the day, then the daily meditation, which was a sermonette loosely based on the Bible reading, and then he would take phone calls.

That was really what the show was about—the phone calls. And that was where he shone.

I could tell he didn't put much time into the daily meditation, because they all sort of sounded similar and never made that much sense. But with the phone calls, people would ask him questions, ask him for advice, tell him their problems. And he would always have an answer for them. He would always tell them what they wanted to hear—or as he put it, what they needed to hear. And then he would pray with them.

Then of course there was the blessing portion of the program. That was when he would ask for money. But he called it the "blessing portion of the program." It was interspersed every fifteen minutes throughout the four-hour show.

He would say, "It's time to make yourself a blessing. There is something you can do. You can give back to God and make for yourself a blessing by sending in a twenty, fifty, or one-hundred-dollar blessing. When you bless God, God blesses you, because God wants me to send you this . . ." and then he would tell them what they were going to get.

It was always some sort of prize. I say "prize" because they reminded me of something you would get from a Cracker Jack box or at the bottom of a cereal box.

Over the years, it would be different things. It could be as simple as a key chain with a picture of Jesus on it to remind you that Jesus is always with you, and when you remember that every moment, that's when the blessings will start to flow. Or it could be a prayer cloth that Pastor Bruce had infused with a personal miracle prayer. All you had to do was kneel down on it and pray, mentioning your specific need or blessing, and then that infused personal miracle prayer from Pastor Bruce would be released. And *that's* when the blessings would start to flow.

Then there was a sin-soaking sponge. It was just a one-inch, flattened, dried-out piece of sponge. If you poured water on it as you confessed your sins, the sponge would grow, soaking up that water and your sins. And guess what—*that's* when the blessings would start to flow. Then there was a vial of pure River of Jordan miracle water, taken from the very spot where Jesus was baptized in the Jordan River. It was a plastic tube, not really a vial, with a little water in it, and you were supposed to tear it open and pour it on your head, and of course *that's* when the blessings would start to flow.

There was a whole catalog of these things, if you can believe it. My dad ordered them by the case. You could pay extra to have the name of the evangelist or the ministry printed on them, so it could be Pastor Bruce's River of Jordan Miracle Water, but my dad never did that.

His was sort of a shoestring operation. He never could afford extra expenses. Even as radio evangelist ministries went, his was pretty lean. He was then the only employee of "The Daily Bread with Pastor Bruce Evangelistic Ministries." He had a P.O. box in Yuma—something about the Arizona laws being more accommodating to his brand of ministry. He'd go three times a week to

Yuma to collect all the blessings, count them, deposit them in the bank there, holding back the cash—people actually sent cash through the mail—stop by the liquor store, drive the forty miles back to Plaster City, where he would start filling all the orders for the miracle blessing prizes.

He didn't make a lot of money, but enough to pay for the airtime and give my mom and me a little more than subsistence living conditions. He didn't care. He drank and preached. That's what he loved to do, and as long as he could afford to keep doing those two things, nothing else mattered much.

He was good at it, too. Well, drinking doesn't take that much talent and I guess you wouldn't really call it preaching, but he could talk. And he had a voice. Every night that I could remember until I was fifteen, I would fall asleep to that voice. It was smooth and comforting, and no matter what kind of problem a caller had, he sounded like he was right there with them and he understood, and when he told them how much God loved them and wanted to bless them, you practically heard God saying it himself.

He promised people all kinds of things. Someone was broke and the bank was going to take their house; he felt led to tell them that an unexpected inheritance was coming. Someone had an inoperable cancer; God was their spiritual surgeon and he could feel him operating as they spoke. The callers would claim they could feel it, too. I guess if it is two o'clock in the morning and the caller is in El Paso, Texas, you can promise them just about anything and never have to worry about whether that promise was kept or not.

At home, he never spoke that way. I never heard that comforting, healing voice. At home when he spoke, he was either in a rage or silly.

By the time I was in my early teens, I just straight-out hated him. I spent my whole life never knowing if he was going to slap me on the back and call me buddy or knock me to the floor. I just knew there was nothing I could do to affect it either way. So

I just did whatever I could to avoid him, which got easier because when I was about fifteen, he started not coming home after his shows. It would go in streaks. He wouldn't be home for two or three days every couple of weeks, and then he would be gone longer and more often. But as much as I hated him, I still listened to him every night. It did give me comfort in a strange way. Even if he was gone a week or more, he was always there every night on the radio.

One night when it was real bad like that—he had been gone longer than ever before—I was listening to him tell this caller who had lost her dog (lost her dog!) that the Lord knew where her dog was, and he felt led to tell her that her dog was OK and would be coming home soon. I just went to the kitchen and grabbed the phone. I didn't even think about it. It was like an involuntary action.

My mom was asleep, so I brought it onto the back porch, sat on the floor, and started dialing the radio station. I had never called the station before, and I only half realized that's what I was doing then. Until I got to the last digit. Then I realized I was calling Pastor Bruce to ask him if my dad was going to come home. And when I realized that I just started bawling. Crying uncontrollably. I just wanted to hear that comforting voice, telling me that the Lord knew where my dad was and that he felt led to tell me he was on his way home. I was crying so hard, I was shaking. No matter how much I wanted to do it, I couldn't make myself dial the last number.

I hung up the phone and cried. I was so angry. I was trying to get myself under control but I was so mad. I hated him so much for making me too scared to ask him a question. Imagine. I was so twisted around that I was too scared to even ask my own dad if he was coming home that night. How could he do that to me? Who could do that to their kid? I never ever wanted to see him again. I prayed and sobbed that if God could ever do *anything,* could ever make *any* miracle happen, then God should make my dad go away forever.

I got up and ran to the studio. The church was just three blocks over from our house. I ran. When I got to the church, it was after four already. I didn't see his car, but I tried the door and it was open. I went to the broadcast booth. Everything was shut down, but the light was on. Maybe he was coming back. I sat down in his chair and saw his bottle and his glass on the table by the microphone. I decided I'd make myself a miracle. I grabbed handfuls of those little plastic packets of River of Jordan miracle water; there was a whole open case of them. My dad said they weren't that popular because people thought they were too much like holy water, which was a Catholic thing. I ripped them open with my teeth and poured a bunch of them in the glass until it was half full and then filled it up the rest of the way from the bottle of Old Granddad and I drank miracle water and whiskeys until the sun came up.

I don't know if it was the River of Jordan water or the whiskey or the mix of the two, but somehow I managed to make myself a miracle. My prayer was answered. I never saw my dad again.

Sometimes I have to talk about the darkness to separate it from the light.

Post-Apocalyptic Praise Song, Part Two

I had another dream vision thing. Well the same one but more. It was about that song. That song. I am beginning to suspect that it was not a dream.

That room where I was being detained with Idiot John (only he wasn't Idiot John anymore) I realized was not a holding room or some cell in the bowels of this mega-church. I realized it was the old church library. I could see from the map mounted next to the door that they probably never used this old library any-more, because there was a large area labeled "Video Library and Contemporary Christian Computer Center." The room I thought was a holding cell was in a section that was shaded gray on the map and labeled simply with the word "Old." As if that was enough to tell anybody everything they needed to know about this part of the building. Old equals bad. (You could hide anything if you just put it in a bag and wrote "Old" on it. The Contemporary Christians would have nothing to do with it.) "Old" is one of those words that became a concept like Uncomfortable, Dis-ease, and Uncertainty—concepts that were now universally avoided and despised.

I know I am beginning to sound like that guy who used to be Idiot John—yeah—he is still in the room. He is back in the cor-ner. In the low light it is hard to see him sitting on the floor, with his legs pulled up tight against his chest like he's trying to wedge himself further into the corner. It's hard to see his face.

He is still there. He stopped talking. He did not talk while I walked around the old library. I picked up this old soft-cover book;

I realized it was *The* Book. I opened the front cover, "Given by Eugene Guilbransen in loving memory of his wife of 46 years, Mildred."

"Don't think it is all over," he said to me. I was so startled when he spoke that I jerked and accidentally ripped the front cover and the dedication page off that old book.

From the corner of the room, he went on. "I will show you everything I have told you is true. You have the proof in your hand. The Contemporary Christian Commission Commission got it all wrong. Everything they've been doing—preaching the Good News of the Kingdom of God to every corner of the globe—didn't work. It didn't work because they reached every single corner of the globe with the wrong news.

"Just look in the book. You don't believe me? Look in Matthew—it's the end of the book—just read the last four sentences of Matthew's story."

I read.

Now the eleven disciples went to Galilee, to the mountain to which Jesus had directed them. When they saw him, they worshiped him; but some doubted. And Jesus came and said to them, all authority in heaven and on earth has been given to me, go therefore and make disciples of all nations, baptizing them in the name of the Father and of the Son and of the Holy Spirit and teaching them to obey everything that I have commanded you. And remember, I am with you always, to the end of the age.

He kept going, "I don't know were to start." He was excited now. I couldn't really see his face, but I could hear the spittle forming in the corners of his mouth.

"I don't even know were to start—I want to tell you about it all. In Jesus' time, you could *doubt*. We are called to make *disciples*. I am with you *always*. What if he didn't need to come back because he was *already* . . . No, no, there are so many things to tell you, but right now there is not much time and I can tell I am frightening you. Here. Just remember this: "The Contemporary Christian Commission Commission started with the wrong commission. They took these last four sentences and distorted them until they became something they could control. But they started in the wrong place. Read chapter 10. It's right there in your hand—read it."

I stared down at my hands. One held the book with its cover torn off. The other held the old cover and old Eugene Guilbransen's dedication page. I turned to chapter 10 and read the passage to myself.

These twelve he sent out—go only to the lost sheep of the house of Israel, and proclaim first to them the good news of the kingdom of God. Proclaim to them that the kingdom of God is near, heal every one of them that are sick, those that are outcasts like the lepers and the poor people, heal them, restore them to their families and proclaim to the family that all of God's children are welcome in the family of God of the new kingdom.

I looked back at him. He looked back at me, nodding like he could hear inside my head and like it proved something.

"But the Contemporary Christians don't hear that text, don't see the mirror. They don't understand what it is telling them—that it is messy. It's not going to be easy to go to the Contemporary Christian Culture and tell them about the New Kingdom when they are in control of the Old Kingdom. It won't be easy to tell them that they are not leading people into the family of God but creating new consumers for the Old Kingdom—the Contemporary Christian Kingdom." This guy is no longer wedged in the corner. Now he is up on one knee in the corner, gesturing crazily with this sweeping upward hand motion, like he is begging me or praying to me.

It is freaking me out.

"'I did not come to bring peace to the world, but a sword.' Get it? Jesus is coming, not to confirm our own creation or to applaud our own understanding. He is coming to hack off the grotesque appendages we have grafted on. Anyone who claims the Contemporary Christian Capitalist Kingdom is not the Kingdom of God will hear about it from their mother and father, their sister and brother—your grandmother will put you on her church's prayer chain; your grandfather will cut you out of the will or kick you out of the country club."

Now in the half-light coming in through the window, I can see his upturned face. When it is not obscured by the shadows from his wild pleading/praying gestures, I can see the spittle from the corners of his mouth gaining critical mass, falling back into his mouth, only to be propelled into the air in this great arc and landing on the book in my hand. Landing on the dedication page. Actual drops of spittle are visible on Mildred's name.

"Jesus was saying his disciples would have to give up their lives—be killed. But they missed it, the Contemporary Christians. Nobody is getting killed here. No one is getting scorned by his family—no one is rocking the boat. No one is asking questions they don't already know the answers to. No one has any doubts. Nobody is one bit uncomfortable about the current state of the house of Israel . . . I mean the Christian church. No one is ill at ease, questioning the great Commission Commission. No one is inconvenienced. There are no dissenters. Everyone is at peace.

"That is why we are launching the Counter Commission Commission: going to every church and asking them to be uncomfortable—to ask questions they do not know the answers to, to come to the Bible and to the church with uncomfortable questions."

Exhausted and weeping, this guy collapses on the floor, which seemed a bit over the top. But I think I understood his point: he and his people, whoever they are, are going to launch a revolution against the forces that control all the power in the world—cultural, religious, political, and financial.

But they are going to do it by asking people to make themselves uncomfortable? Well, at least you can't be arrested for that. But come on. This seems ridiculous.

But then I remember a Ministers Convention I attended. And I remember having an identical experience at least three different times. I would strike up some casual conversation with one of the other ministers, and we would get to talking about our churches and they would tell me, "We are just laid back—we try to create a place where people feel comfortable—you know, just come as you are. Do you know, when I preach, I don't even wear a tie. I just sit on a stool and talk to people from my heart."

All these different pastors are telling me this exact same thing, in an attempt to show me how progressive, authentic, and Post-Modern they are. Really, one preacher from Atlanta told me he didn't wear a tie as an example of how his worship service is Post-Modern.

I don't even wear a tie. I just sit on a stool and share. I don't even wear a tie. Like the absence of a tie is a universally recognizable good, a Platonic form of authentic Contemporary Christian communication. And the stool? You think I am making this up. *When I preach I don't even wear a tie—I just sit on a stool and talk.* What is the deal with the stool? Is there a place where you can trade in your tie for a stool? You walk up to the counter and give them your tie, they give you a stool, and suddenly you are a Post-Modern minister.

Finally, after the I-don't-know-how-many-millionth minister said, *you know, when I preach I don't even wear a tie, I just . . .* I burst out, "Why? Why?" I remember shouting to keep him from saying *stool*—knowing it would send me into a homicidal frenzy.

"Well," he said, looking at me kind of hurt, "I just want everyone to feel comfortable."

That's when I realized—it is true. Everything the guy was saying was true. Everything the minivan people said is true.

The Contemporary Christian police/usher/ex-professional sports guy came back and let me out of the library. He said I was free to go. And I said, "What about the minivan?" And he said, "There are more important things to worry about," and just left me standing in the hallway.

I looked back into the library where the other guy who was no longer Idiot John was, but he had disappeared. So I ran. Quietly.

I went down halls, up stairs, around and through breezeways, until I started to hear a dull kind of rumbling sound. I followed it as it got louder and louder. It had that kind of chaotic but massive feel of a large crowd in a gym or a convention hall. Then I went through a set of double doors and right into the midst of a large crowd in a gym or a convention hall. The place was huge. There were easily seven thousand people there.

Everybody was dressed causally: khakis, golf shirt, no ties. Except this one guy. The place was crowded and people were all standing packed together. Except around him. People kept their distance from him, as if they didn't want anyone to think they were with him. This guy's fashion infractions weren't limited to his tie. He wore a three-piece suit made of some wrinkle-free fabric, which had somehow managed to become wrinkled, thus guaranteeing that the wrinkles would never come out.

As I was noticing how this guy was sort of an outcast, I looked around and noticed a similar people-free zone had formed around me. So I went over and stood by the wrinkle-free suit guy. As I did, the lights went down and a speaker came out with a stool and a cordless mike, sat down, and began to talk. "I am sorry to report that the world did not end. We have tried our best but it simply keeps going on. And despite our best efforts, it looks like Jesus is not coming back."

There was no huge reaction from the thousands of delegates there, just a collective exhalation of hopelessness.

You see this wasn't really news to any of them. The rumors had been circulating for days that the Commission was going to formally announce that the world was not over. I heard several people in the crowd mention what a shame it was that the world did not end, after they had put so much hard work into it. This must have been the prevailing feeling because the speaker then announced that because everyone had worked so hard, even though the world did not end and Jesus was not going to return, they were going to sing the song anyway as a sign of their faith and a celebration of their hard work.

The Praise Team came up. The rear projection screens came down, and they all closed their eyes and sang like it was the end of the world.

I had just closed my eyes and raised my hands when the wrinkle-free suit guy grabbed my arm and pulled me close and put his lips to my ear and said to me. "What does it mean 'if you lose your life you will find it'? What does it take to realize that your convictions have changed your status in the world? What strength of character is required? What do you do when you are beginning to understand the implications of what you believe? When you hear the words that make your muscles burn and your mind leap forward in an endless chain of possibilities and logical causes and effects—if X then Y, if Y then Z? What exactly do you do? When it is no longer possible to look at everyone around you, doing things and wearing things and buying things and talking about things on the television and what everyone on the television is wearing and buying and doing and talking about—when it is no longer possible to look at everyone around you and say, *that is me.* That is me. I am like that. I do those things. I wear those things.

"When, instead, you are compelled to say, and jolted by the compulsion, *that is not me.* I am *not* like that. I no longer belong where I once belonged.

"When your world starts to end, what do you do?"

I turned to him (and this makes me think it was a dream because everyone started singing louder yet it's also perfectly quiet and nobody paid attention to the two of us) and I said to him, "What do you do when you feel the world starting to end?"

"There are choices," he said pushing his lips deeper into my ear, "and it is possible to make the wrong choices, and there are dire consequences for making the wrong choices.

"When your world starts to end, when your life starts to slip away—you can stop it. You can grab your old life, hold it close to you and keep it. Then you can pretend that the experience of almost losing your life, the panic and exhilaration you felt when your world almost ended—you can pretend that experience *was* the transformation. And you can pretend that the life you are living is not the same old life, but the new life—that the Old Kingdom has passed away and the Kingdom of God is near."

"What are the consequences if people make that choice?" I asked.

"The world turns out like this."

"What else can you do?"

"If you let the world end? If you let the life you knew slip away? If you lose your life?"

"Yeah." Just then I started to feel this weird sensation like I was sinking or drowning, like everything was going black and I was going to lose consciousness. I asked him straight out, "Is the world going to end?"

And I'll tell you what he told me: "What if the world ends one person at a time? And what if the New World begins one person at a time? And what if you bring each person over the line, help them die, by wasting time with them, listening to them, taking advice from them, or eating with them at a dinner table—a communion table."

I lost consciousness. I woke up in my office with the phone ringing and my car keys in my hand. My journal was open on the floor. I answered the phone. There was someone there but they didn't say anything. I looked down at my journal then something caught my eye. I noticed my office door was ajar.

journal entry
(a top priority for
your wednesday)

There was a meeting today. This one I had to go to. I got a phone call from three different Coaches and two Support Team members and received one memo marked: "A top priority for your Wednesday."

The meeting turned out to be something between an intervention and a firing. At first I didn't really get it. I didn't even know that I was the focus of the meeting. There was coffee and pastry. There was one chair open between Our Senior Pastor and the Lead Coach for Counseling and Staff Wellness. I was so distracted by the off-gassing from the carpet and ceiling tiles and every other veneered, glued, or molded piece of furniture and feature. I was trying to keep my mind from pursuing the thought that this synthetic smell was a kind of nerve gas for the soul—something the Conspiracy developed to hasten the transition from being a normal, questioning, thinking, hopeful individual to being an encouraging team player with an unacknowledged reservoir of fear.

It first occurred to me that something was up when the Lead Coach to my right put his hand on shoulder, gave my neck a reassuring little squeeze and said, "Would you dedicate our time together to the Lord?"

All eyes on me. All heads unbowed. The looks of all my colleagues, eyes filled with self-pity and soft caring, came off as a really nice lynch mob about to do the right thing. Eyes open, head unbowed, I stuttered, "Lord? We dedicate our time to you. Ah, amen." Caught a little off-guard by my TV-style praying, some closed their eyes and dipped their heads belatedly.

The Lead Coach's hand was still on my shoulder (he kept it there the entire meeting). I looked over to Our Senior Pastor, who looked at me and put his hand on my other shoulder and said, "So, how are you doing? I mean *really* doing?"

I didn't know what to say. My left leg started bouncing up and down.

"Can we share with you what we see?" said the Lead Coach.

I nodded my head up and down briefly in synch with my leg. The Coach turned his head to the Ministry Team—all the Coaches and Wranglers and Navigators and Master Encouragers assembled around the table. Golf shirts of every imaginable shade shifted in their chairs.

One leaned forward, a pale yellow: "What I see is that you really care. You care a lot." A pastel blue quickly added, "You work really hard." Many nods of agreement, "I worry about your self-care," from a tomato-soup red.

"I think we all do, buddy," from Our Senior Pastor (his hand, too, still on my shoulder). "One of the things we do here in this gathering is care for each other when someone forgets to care for themselves. That's a priority for us." More nods of agreement.

That is when I understood. The signs were all there—the hand on the shoulder (not one but two), the caring, the buddy— I was being fired.

"We'd like to encourage you to take some extended self-care time."

I was being fired in a very nice way.

For the first time in the meeting, my mind started working a little bit. It fought to shake of the effects of the Conspiracy's numbing soul gas. So many thoughts and questions simultaneously: How long is extended? What will I do? But wait—it is working, the revolution has struck a blow. This is no time to go quietly, it is time to strike harder. I must be allowed to preach one more sermon. I'll tell the people why they are trying to get rid of me. I wonder if I get to keep my benefits?

Our Senior Pastor looked into my eyes as if he had been reading my mind and said, "Of course you'll be able to keep your benefits while you're on leave of absence. This is really a great opportunity to get reoriented. And you have my word that you will not be forgotten at this gathering."

I opened my mouth, but my mind's struggle against the soul gas was lost. "Thank you," I said, and got up and left.

post-rapture radio
part three

A new Heaven
and a new earth

From Lamblove's commentary on the Book of Revelation

consuming the future for
short-term existential gain

Everybody wants a plan, a sequence, a timeline, rules, categories, a measuring rod. This is the business of the Contemporary Christian Culture Conspiracy. It is the illusion of progress. It is about improvement. Self-improvement. Growing. Growing a church, growing your spiritual gifts, growing your own wealth. The Revelation of Jesus Christ to St. John pulls back the veil to expose it all as a lie—as the beast, the Anti-Christ.

It is granting something meaning that is meaningless. It is making something important that is not important. It is making something sacred that is not sacred. It is making the *Anti* the Christ, worshiping the Anti—the no-thing.

When Revelation is read as a timeline that one can use to plot the progress to the end of the world, it becomes a product for Contemporary Christian Culture consumption. A product has no meaning. The whole of the book is a telling and retelling of how the Roman Empire looks to one who has not been assimilated by it. It contains a constant call to repent and come out of Babylon. It says, you think the Empire is comfortable? You think wearing a toga with a fish logo on it is bearing witness? Wake up! Hear what the Savior has to say to the churches!

The amazing, almost incomprehensible, thing about the book occurs in chapter 21. After all these cycles of warning and judgment and calls for repentance, calls to come out of Babylon and live in the Kingdom of God—the opposite happens. The churches don't come out of Babylon, so God brings the Kingdom to them.

Then I saw a new heaven and a new earth; for the first heaven and the first earth had passed away, and the sea was no more. And I saw the holy city, new Jerusalem, coming down out of heaven from God, prepared as a bride adorned for her husband; and I heard a great voice from the throne saying, "Behold, the dwelling of God is with men. He will dwell with them and they shall be his people and God himself will be with them" (Rev. 21:1–3).

This is it. This is the true story. Babylon and the New Jerusalem are not places; they are relationships. The Contemporary Christian Culture Conspiracy does not want us to know this. They don't want people to see that Contemporary Culture is Babylon and that the church and Babylon are hopelessly enmeshed. They would be shocked at the suggestion that their values are in any way similar to the values of Contemporary Culture. In truth, the Babylonian relationship is what defines the Conspiracy. But it is not just the Conspiracy—we all live in the Babylonian relationship. We cannot free ourselves from the evil that we love. We cannot get ourselves to leave Babylon, so God comes to get us. The New Jerusalem comes down from heaven and God dwells with us.

Editor's Comment

....

The following journal entry and next two sermons make it clear that Lamblove, in spite of his sometimes-stated desire to be fired, feels lost without his position at the church. It has always been my contention that his rebel stance was motivated by his feelings of not belonging. At least when he was working within what he calls Contemporary Christian Culture, he belonged a little. After being given a leave of absence, he does not even have that. Instead he is alone and sinks into self-pity and even questions his revolution. It has become clear to him that no one is going to rise up and drive the cashiers out of the temple. It must have been sobering to realize that after all his "revolutionary" preaching, in the end no one was paying attention. No one cared. He wasn't let go because his firebrand proclamation offended anyone or because he struck a deathblow with his sword of truth, but because he seemed kind of mopey and depressed.

This is where he should just walk away and let the Contemporary Christian Culture be what it is. If he doesn't want any part of it, fine. Move on. But of course he stays. But I'm ambivalent about how to present the next few pieces. It's simply not clear what Lamblove intended. I thought about just removing the scriptures and presenting them all as journal entries with no comment but decided to leave the scriptures in. Maybe he started out to write a sermon and found himself writing for another audience—possibly for himself. Lamblove's apparent need to write sermons, even though he no longer had a congregation to preach them to, testifies to how much of his identity came from his calling. Or maybe not; maybe he just needs to write to figure things out. Maybe it helps.

journal entry
(what does it matter?)

I feel weird. I feel kind of afraid or ashamed but mixed together. Aframed or ashade. I am trying to talk out loud more. It is funny, I realized that I talk more now at my lame part-time job at the coffee shop than I did as a preacher. I guess it is because I don't have to talk about anything important. Or I don't have to weigh what everybody says, considering what they really mean and what the ramifications are with regard to the revolution. At the coffee shop someone says, "I'll have a large dark roast to go." And I say, "Room for cream?" It is a question. I can ask questions that need to be asked and answered. There is no grey area. There is only coffee.

I would talk when I preached, of course. But any other time I would just hurry to my office and pray I didn't meet anyone on the way. It seemed dangerous to talk to anyone because it seemed like that is a way that they sort of indoctrinate you. Like they say the same meaningless things over and over, and then you start to think that is what it means to talk to another person. It is the way TV works. It is the way culture works. The same vacuous things happen and are said over and over, and then you start to think that is what life is made of. You start to care—actually care about how much money you'll save. Care about the final episode when the two seemingly incongruous characters will be wed. Care about a scandal.

That's it. That right there proves that the Contemporary Christian Culture Conspiracy has subsumed secular popular culture. "A scandal" has come to mean the opposite. That which should scandalize does not, and that which is commonplace is sold as a scandal. Scandal becomes just a different product. A pop star is arrested for beating his wife! Detectives are saying there were drugs involved! That is a scandal? A scandal, by definition, is when someone acts in a way that brings shame and offends the cultural norm. The pop star offends no one. The pop star feels no shame. It is the cultural norm that pop stars get up to reprehensible behavior. It is part of being a pop star. It is not offensive; it is titillating. It compels listeners to tune in and buy the CD.

What is truly scandalous has become commonplace: churches showing previews for a Hollywood movie during a worship service or God's son going to his death without defending himself? Those are scandals. But these things are not considered, not even noticed. Where is the shame? Where is the offense?

I thought I could bring the true scandals to the congregation. I would lay these scandals bare and the people would feel the offense, and having felt the offense, they would rise up and act. But instead I am fired, I think, for not wearing a golf shirt. No one really cared about what I was saying. It was more like they didn't even hear me when I was talking.

That is why I am trying to talk out loud more. I think I have something wrong with me. "Can you hear me?" I say that out loud a lot. But I never say it when anyone else is around. So I don't know if I can be heard. I know I can hear myself. But I don't know if the sounds come out right when I'm in front of other people. When I say, "Room for cream?" people seem to hear it.

I have started moving furniture into my basement. Not to store it but so I have a place to sit and something to sleep on. I feel like I should be down there. I am starting to wonder if it is just me—and not the rest of the world—that is confused.

But on the other hand I feel like there is something different about talking out loud freely to people who can hear me and understand what I am saying in the coffee shop and talking out loud urgently and furtively to people who do not seem to hear me or understand me when I preach a sermon. The latter seems more important and more true. True, you see—I said true. I think maybe what is true always seems quite like gibberish.

I guess while I like speaking out loud, I miss the gibberish.

Editor's Comment

....

I don't see how Lamblove could have meant this next piece to be a sermon, even though he starts out with scripture. I guess he might have written it to work out his thoughts. Or it could have been a journal entry that slipped out of sequence. I'm calling it a sermon because he included it with his sermons, but, as I say, Lamblove's categories seem to be collapsing.

sermon
why is evil funny?

MARK 1:21–28

And they went into Capernaum; and immediately on the Sabbath he entered the synagogue and taught. And they were astonished at his teaching, for he taught them as one who had authority, and not as the scribes. And immediately there was in their synagogue a man with an unclean spirit; and he cried out, "What have you to do with us, Jesus of Nazareth? Have you come to destroy us? I know who you are, the Holy One of God." But Jesus rebuked him, saying, "Be silent, and come out of him!" And the unclean spirit, convulsing him and crying with a loud voice, came out of him. And they were all amazed, so that they questioned among themselves, saying, "What is this? A new teaching! With authority he commands even the unclean spirits, and they obey him." And at once his fame spread everywhere throughout all the surrounding region of Galilee.

. . . .

Evil Kinevel [Evel Knievel] wears white—white leather, granted, but it's still white. And he doesn't pretend to be evil at all. He is good. He is entertaining, fun to watch. "Evil" just sounds cool and it rhymes with "Kinevel" (from *Evil Kinevel and Other Not Evil Things*).✻

He wanted evil to be worse than it was. That's what he was obsessed with. That and this dirty sock. There was a dirty sock on

---

✻ After an exhaustive search, I have concluded that this book does not exist. Rev. Rathbun, I can say with certainty, is making this reference up. It is a calculated fabrication, as is much of the premise from which he writes.

top of the television in his room. A dirty sock sort of semi-balled up to the heel, with the toe hanging over the left corner of the TV screen.

He sat on his bed, leaning against the wall in the middle of this sleepless stew of twisted sheet and blanket, yesterday's newspaper, empty Diet Coke cans, a Japanese comic book, and a volume of French cultural criticism, all of which (he couldn't even admit to himself) he had absolutely no interest in.

He had barely moved from this position since taking a leave of absence from his job, surrounded by this clutter and pages and papers and notes. A journal lay open on the floor. Every time he looked at these things, it was like reading someone else's mind. It felt like he had been here for a thousand years.

He just sat staring at the muted television, not paying any attention to the transvestites fighting, Hawkeye's humorous self-righteousness, or the countless opportunities to enter the exciting career fields of medical/dental technology, computer graphics, and Web design, or the miraculous opportunity to grow his own wealth.

His mind was somewhere else. His mind was on evil. Why couldn't evil be worse than it was? Why couldn't it be clearly discernable and really horrifying (or at least really bad)? Why couldn't it be like a beast rising out of the sea with ten horns and seven heads and a blasphemous name and have a mortal wound upon its head? Why couldn't evil be like that? Evil should be recognizable to everyone. It should matter. If evil really existed, it should have a clear effect on his life. For that matter, what did evil have to do with him? How did evil affect his life?

He knew there was systematic evil: self-obsessed capitalists who continually profit from the manipulation of those with less power or knowledge, self-obsessed nationalists driven to destroy the other team. He knew there was individual evil: people acting out of a cocktail of self-obsession and rage at not getting what they thought they should have. But he couldn't imagine that these people acted out of pure evil or out of a desire to do something evil. They acted, he was sure, in ways they thought were justifiable, understandable, perhaps even reasonable, and yes, even good.

He wanted evil to be pure. Something you could see. You could say, "Hey there's the evil, let's get it." You could fight it. Call an exorcist. Call on Jesus. Jesus could meet evil in the desert, in the synagogue, at the water's edge, on the plain of Megiddo. Jesus could drive it out. Where is that kind of evil? Where is that kind of Jesus? This is the question that had lodged itself in his head and started the obsession.

Sitting in bed with his brain in neutral, staring at the ceiling, opening and closing one eye to make the overhead light fixture jump back and forth, he felt this question impose itself. A memory of a question really. When he was a little kid he had asked his mom, "Mom, what does Jesus do?"

"Jesus brings the Good News of the Kingdom of God and defeats evil."

He was impressed. She had the answer right there. No hesitation—Jesus brings the Good News of the Kingdom of God and defeats evil. It seemed powerful. It sounded like what Jesus would do. But now when he thought about it, it just made him mad. *Jesus brings the Good News of the Kingdom of God and defeats evil.* What the hell does that mean? What is the Good News? That's totally meaningless. Defeats evil? That's an answer to a question about a superhero.

He decided to scrap his plans to spend the day focusing on the overhead light fixture and direct his attention to this question. Forget this nebulous notion of "good news." He had given up on believing there was anything even resembling good news a long time ago. But evil—that is where he focused. What is evil? Real evil, pure evil?

There were some classic examples: Pol Pot, slavery, Hitler (everyone always pointed to Hitler). But even then, the evil Hitler had long disappeared, replaced by the cartoon Hitler, the Hitler that was brought out to end an argument being lost ("Well, what about Hitler?"). Or the Hitler that inspires neo-Nazi punks as a television plot point when the writers occasionally wanted to lend some moral weight to the lead character's chasing and shooting and arresting. Either way, both Hitlers were just devices that were far removed from any actual evil.

The television screen flashed brightly and drew his attention to the sock. He could not remember how it had gotten there or how long it had been there. It seemed like a long time. He could remember it being there yesterday. He thought he could remember it being there last Tuesday when he watched *Buffy the Vampire Slayer*. But he could not remember when he first noticed it, or why it was still there.

Why did it seem like such a hassle to get up, take the sock off the TV, and put it with the other dirty clothes? What kind of person, he thought, watches TV for weeks with a dirty sock blocking part of the screen? It was irritating, distracting. But he had learned that after a while it could be ignored, forgotten. It would just sort of blend in, but then something would happen and it would catch his attention again. He did try to knock it off by throwing another sock at it. But he missed. Then the commercial was over and he got caught up in the show again and forgot about it. And so he just sat there with only one sock on.

If evil can be overcome, he figured, it has to be identified. To this he dedicated himself.

What is evil? He was naturally suspicious, and knew the question was not easily answered. Because evil, he realized quickly, has a way of looking exactly the way you expect it to look. If you are politically conservative, it looks like liberal teachers attempting to corrupt the moral values of the youth with every lesson plan. If you are Cuban, it looks like the United States trying to destroy your country and steal your children. If evil in any way resembles those you are in opposition to or are unfamiliar with—those you don't know or understand or are scared of—those notions of evil immediately have to come into question.

The world seemed to present only two options when it came to evil. (Now, granted, when he spoke of "the options the world presented," he meant the options the media presented—because he rarely left his house and spent most of his time watching TV, and occasionally reading. And though he didn't talk to too many people, he couldn't believe they would be much different from those he saw on television or came across in books and magazines.) The two options for evil were either entertaining evil or boring evil.

Neither presentation of evil was convincing. Just the opposite: they distanced him from any idea of pure evil. The Entertaining Evil was always resolved; no matter what mayhem had occurred, some-one was left smiling. In recent years, horror films had even stopped pretending evil existed and they turned into horror comedies. And what about Doctor Evil? Just combining the word "evil" with another word made it funny. Evil was funny. Anything presented as evil was quickly forgotten after the credits rolled.

Boring Evil was probably closer to the real thing, but who could tell? It was all words—words about something really bad that happened to someone else (or a lot of someone elses), someplace else. It was all facts and figures—scientific studies about crime statistics, nuclear waste, and deformed frogs. If he did get past the dead delivery of the information and begin to understand what was actually being said, it quickly became overwhelming and numbed him from any immediate sense of evil.

He had a sort of vague feeling that the real evil was all around him, that he had lived his life in the middle of it, surrounded by it, like everyone. That maybe he could not see evil as it really is because like everyone else he knew it so well. He thought that if someone came from another world or at least another country, they could see how it surrounded everything and how it really looked, and they would be horrified. What if what that outsider felt was evil was what made everyone else feel comfortable? But that vague feeling and fleeting thoughts left him completely. He wanted clarity and purity. He wanted to see it and feel it.

What about pure evil? He thought. He didn't know any evil people. He knew he wasn't evil. Early on in his obsession, he decided he would try to become evil, but it seemed like such a hassle, so he forgot about it. He wanted pure evil. If a demon would appear, fine. And if Jesus would come and defeat it, all the better. And while he was at it, how about bringing a little of that Good News with him?

Short of that, he had concluded that, like the Good News, there was no such thing as evil.

A slight motion caught his eye. He looked up.

The sock had fallen farther, covering more of the TV screen. He took the remaining sock off his foot and threw at the TV to knock the sock off. He missed.

sermon

separation in light of personal experience

JOHN 15:1–12

I am the true vine, and my Father is the vinedresser. Every branch of mine that bears no fruit, he takes away, and every branch that does bear fruit he prunes, that it may bear more fruit. You are already made clean by the word which I have spoken to you. Abide in me, and I in you. As the branch cannot bear fruit by itself, unless it abides in the vine, neither can you, unless you abide in me. I am the vine, you are the branches. He who abides in me, and I in him, he it is that bears much fruit, for apart from me you can do nothing. If a man does not abide in me, he is cast forth as a branch and withers; and the branches are gathered, thrown into the fire and burned. If you abide in me, and my words abide in you, ask whatever you will, and it shall be done for you. By this my Father is glorified that you bear much fruit, and so prove to be my disciples. As the Father has loved me, so have I loved you; abide in my love. If you keep my commandments, you will abide in my love, just as I have kept my Father's commandments and abide in his love. These things I have spoken to you, that my joy may be in you, and that your joy may be full.

This is my commandment, that you love one another as I have loved you.

. . . .

Since it happened, Malcolm had been experimenting with separation. It started as the result of a recent memory. He remembered sitting in the kitchen, three days earlier, at the small table when he received the phone call.

After they had hung up, he, for whatever reason, did not move. He kept the phone pressed against the side of his head. He did not move, but only increased the pressure, flattening his ear against his skull, listening harder to the silence. Only when the blood began to pound in his ear did he realize what he was doing, but still found it impossible to move or release the pressure.

He made a decision to hang up the phone—willed himself to hang up the phone—but his thoughts seemed separate from the rest of him; they could not initiate any action.

He sat frozen, staring straight ahead at a potted cherry-tomato plant sitting in the middle of the table. He planned to put it in his garden. His eyes fixed on a small green fruit at the end of the largest branch. Impulsively, he reached out with his left hand and broke the branch off. This action, odd and inexplicable as it was, freed him, and he hung up the phone, laid the branch with its small fruit on the table, and got up and went to lie down on his bed.

For whatever reason three days later, lying on his bed, the memory surfaced. He got up and went to the kitchen. It was still there of course, and for the most part unchanged. The leaves were wilted but still green and the fruit only somewhat darker.

"What happens," he thought, "when things become detached?" And though not a scientist, he decided on a series of experiments to separate parts from their whole. What would happen if everything in his life became detached? So he set about separating things as he came across them.

He cut the cord off the toaster. He went into his back yard and pulled the leaves and the petals from his flowers, broke branches from his trees, took the grill from his barbecue, and snapped off the aluminum legs. Making several trips, he gathered up all the pieces and brought them into the kitchen. He laid everything out on the floor so he might observe over time what would happen to each individual item.

His kitchen became the laboratory in which he conducted his experiments. He laid out newly separated items, recorded their conditions in a notebook, and observed and noted their changes every day.

He went into every room in his house, preparing items for his experiment. From his closet, he cut legs off his pants and sleeves from shirts; he ripped the lining from his suits. He took an axe to his couch, separating the sides and back from the bench. He brought all the pieces into the kitchen.

Every day new items: computer and stereo (separating individual wires and circuit boards), all the houseplants, lawn furniture. He shut off the water and disassembled the plumbing that ran to the shower. He took off the showerhead, the faucet, the handle. He removed the pipes under the bathroom sink, took out the drain stopper, took off the faucet and the handles, and then separated the sink from the wall. He then set about prying and breaking the ceramic tiles off the wall. He spent half a day carrying the separated parts that were the whole of his bathroom to the kitchen, laying them out and recording them in the notebook.

His answering matching was full and would no longer take new messages. No one came by, since he hadn't returned their phone calls. And in light of what had happened, they didn't want to intrude if he chose to be alone.

He went out on his front steps daily only to retrieve the mail and the newspaper, which he would immediately begin separating into parts. He took the bills from their envelopes, ripped the plastic film from the address window of the envelope, and tore off the stamp. He separated the front page of the newspaper from the back page, the sports section from the TV listings, the arts and culture from the religion section. Then he shredded them all.

Everything he came across, he separated and brought to the kitchen, which was now a tangle of building materials, scraps of metal, and rotting fruit. He had separated bananas from their skins and apples from their seeds; foul-smelling chicken thigh meat he had scraped from the bones; on top of this, precariously stacked, were withered and dried-out tree branches, chair backs, wire, pipes, clothes. The pile was no longer any good for clinical observation, as it was difficult to find an individual item from day to day.

But even before that, he had given up taking notes. Realizing that each page in the notebook was bound together, he promptly ripped them out and threw them on the pile.

He had to pick his way through the mess, balancing precariously on top of the heap and stepping through some places in the pile that were nearly waist deep. He slipped and fell into the stove, which he set about dismantling—taking off the door, unscrewing the hinges, lifting off the burners and the top.

It was only a natural progression to look next to his own body. He started with his hair; then with a pair of scissors he had to reassemble, he cut off his eyelashes and made only marginally successful attempts at his eyebrows.

He wondered, if he were still keeping track, what changes in his own body he might record. Was he withering away like the organic materials? Or was he just lifeless and hard like so many inanimate objects on his kitchen heap?

He looked at the scissors in his right hand and next at the fingers on his left. He cut his pinkie, ring finger, and, with some effort, his thumb off at the first joint.

Then, whether from hunger or loss of blood, he lost consciousness.

The investigators could not conclude specifically what had caused the fire.

There were so many possibilities: the bare wires from the toaster, blender, and coffee-maker dangling from the socks, the exposed pilot light from the dismantled stove. All of this was surrounded by a three-foot-thick pile of potential fuels—dried branches, junk mail, newspapers, and furniture. The entire house was lost.

The neighbor who had found him barely conscious on the front steps called an ambulance but could not think of anyone to call to tell what hospital he had been taken to.

Editor's Comment
....

Lamblove has always had a taste for the bizarre in
his sermons but rarely has he been so autobiographical
in any writing of his that I've found. This next
sermon-like piece reads more like a journal-entry
description of his total collapse. (I'm calling it a
journal entry to avoid confusion.)

Lamblove has often used strange metaphors, but
his use of the fire in the conclusion of "Separation
in Light of Personal Experience" is, I think, literal.
The following piece also ends with a fire. Those two
pieces taken together (I just can't call them
sermons), juxtaposed with several lines from his journal
at around the same time, convince me that he
actually burned down his house. It is hard to say
if it was accidental or deliberate.

What is interesting about these two pieces
is that while they both end in fire, they conclude
very differently. In "Separation," Lamblove seems to
be addressing his own feelings of failure regarding
the revolution. It is surprising how much the loss
of his job has affected him. Being cut off from the
institution※ that he railed against has left him,
seemingly, with nothing. "Mercy Machine" finds Lamblove's
world once again filled with people. The fire in
"Separation" was like Armageddon; the fire in "Mercy
Machine" seems very different.

※ I think it is a complete misunderstanding to say
institution here. Congregation—people—would be much clearer.
The people happen to be in the institution; the people are
assimilated into the empire. Can one be separated from
the institution and not be separated from the people?

But what is Lamblove playing at? Saying, "I am not going to tell you who this happened to"—his very first line—is akin to saying that it happened to him. So this is not really a sermon at all. Where is the scripture text? It is not necessarily a journal entry either. It is as if Lamblove is trying his hand at a short story. What I find interesting about this sermon/story is that the crazy preacher in the story is not himself. He is clearly in the story as the observer, the reporter. It is odd to see him, in essence, reflecting on himself. The character of Pastor Nick has some similarities to Lamblove, but there also seems to be some distance between who Lamblove is (or I should say, who I have concluded Lamblove is, based on my observations) and who Pastor Nick is. It is as if Lamblove is trying to understand who he is by re-conceiving of himself as another. He is trying to find meaning in the burning down of his house. He examines himself by creating a character that is not himself and ascribing to that character actions that are similar to actions he has taken in his life. He then rewrites his own story by telling Pastor Nick's story in an attempt to explain what has happened to him. Whether this is a healthy and successful technique, I cannot tell. It could very easily be seen as delusional. Lamblove, being lost in a deep depression after having been fired and realizing that his revolution is nothing more than an inability to negotiate the culture he is part of, isolates himself and ends up either purposely or accidentally burning down his house. I think there must certainly have been alcohol involved. So in a drunken depression, he burns down his house. Instead of facing that sad reality, he makes it into a metaphor for transformation and redemption. How is that healthy?

~~Sermon~~

Mercy Machine

Journal Entry
(Mercy Machine)

I'm not going to tell you who this happened to. I am just going to tell you *that* it happened and I am going to tell *what* happened.

I can tell you what happened because I saw some of it, and I heard about all of it. Just for the purposes of telling you this story—because it is easier to tell and listen to a story when the main person in the story has a name—just because of that, I am going to tell you that his name was Mortimer Quindelson. No, that is a dumb name. Nicholas, yeah, Nick. Pastor Nick. He is a pastor.

Nick is a bit *off.* OK, maybe not off. Maybe eccentric is a better word. Maybe I should just say that he has ideas about the world—about the church mostly, but I guess they are about the world, too. So Nick is a bit eccentric. OK, really he is crazy, but in a good way.

The first time I saw the machine, it wasn't finished. It was just barely started, but he showed me the drawings and told me how all the pieces would go together. He told me how it would work.

He showed it to me as the result of a conversation we had at this coffee shop where I work part time. And when I am not working there I hang out there a lot. (All the people who go there seem to hang out there a lot.) Nick was sitting at a table near mine, and he had his notebook out. (He always has his notebook out. So do most of the people there. I guess I do, too. That is the kind of place it is.) Because our tables are so close, I can hear him whisper in a sort of under-the-breath, coffee-breath tone, "John's got the water; Jesus has got the fire. John's got the water; Jesus has got the fire. John's got the water; Jesus has got the fire." So I look up and look over at Pastor Nick, and Pastor Nick looks up and looks over at me and then smiles, like he just realized that he was saying that out loud and not in his head. He makes an apologetic move of his head and gestures with one hand, first slightly to his notebook and then slightly to me by way of explanation and starts to say something but then stops and just smiles. To indicate that I understand, I say, "John's got the water; Jesus has got the fire?" Nick nods his head and says, "Yeah," and stifles a giggle.

I put down my pen and say, "What are you working on, Reverend?" I call him reverend in a kind of joking way, but also to show him a little respect, even though I know he doesn't work at a church anymore. And because I do respect him.

Nick says, "Oh you know, I'm just trying to figure some things out." I say, "Oh I know. We all are." I say that because this is how we talk at the coffee shop. Make contact but don't really get into some one else's business, especially the business in somebody's notebook. Then Nick darts his head forward and toward me and says, "I'm making something, building something, and I'm trying to figure out how to build it. I've never built anything before so it is kind of hard." He pauses. "Do you want to know what I'm building?"

"Yeah, oh yeah, sure," I say, because if someone does want to tell you about the business in their notebook, it is only polite to listen—and then hope it isn't poetry.

"Come here," he says. I get up and sit down at his table; he turns his open notebook around to face me and pushes it across the table. I squint and look, and while intriguing, it's not obvious what the contraption is. Pastor Nick knows this so he tells me, "It's a mercy machine."

"A mercy machine?"

"Yeah," he says, "exactly. It is an automated individual liturgical device."

Now, I need to tell you so you know, when I said Nick was crazy I didn't really mean he was crazy—not clinically, anyway—and when I said he was a pastor but isn't anymore, I didn't mean it in the sense that he used to be a pastor back in the sixties on a hippie commune and too much of the Timothy Leary got to him so he is not a pastor anymore. What I mean is that until very recently, he was one of the up-and-coming new church leaders at a multi-staff church in the western suburbs, but he quit—or was fired or let go. I don't know, but whatever it was, I think it was the result of Pastor Nick being crazy in a good way.

Nick starts to tell me about the mercy machine and then he stops. His eyes tell me he has left, and when he comes back he says, "Do you want to see it?"

I say, "Yeah," because it seems like the kind of crazy I like.

"Come on." He grabs his notebook and shoves it in his bag.

"Now?" I say.

"Yeah, now." So I gather up my stuff and say, "Let's go." Because people who spend a lot of time in coffee shops are people that don't have a lot else going on and can run off in the middle of the afternoon to see a partially finished automated individual liturgical device.

"I'll drive," Pastor Nick says. We get in his nineties-era, brown minivan. I buckle up and look over my shoulder. The back seats have been removed; the space is filled with wood and scrap metal and jugs of purified water and cans of gas. The minivan smells a little like gas.

"Nick, what's the gas for?"

"The fire."

I tell him it seems more like he is building a judgment machine, not a mercy machine. He says, "The more I read the book, the less I can tell them apart." He starts the engine and drives. He starts telling me the answer to a question that for some reason hadn't entered my mind: Why is Pastor Nick making a mercy machine?

"The church is bankrupt," he begins. "The church is bank-rupt, shallow, hollow, dead, with no truth in it. The leaders who control the church are treacherous, shallow, hollow, dead. Dead with no life left in them. They are commodifiers of the gospel, dis-torting it to make it a product that is palpable to a shallow, hol-low, dead culture with no truth left in it. They are incapable of administering the sacraments of the church because they don't even remember what they are really about. For example, at my former place of employment, when I taught the Baptism Prepara-tion classes, I got in a lot of trouble for refusing to include the final session—the one where you helped the Baptism Candidates decide on the best package.

"The standard package came free of charge and included a baptism certificate and a candle to commemorate the event. We were to offer the standard package but to point out that it didn't provide much in the way of 'artifacting' the event. In order to make the event more real for the candidates, it was recommended that they at least choose the 'Ethiopian' package, named for the Ethiopian eunuch that Phillip baptized on the side of the road. This package included a frame for the certificate and the candidate's name in gold on the candle. Hardly anyone chooses this one, and I always suspected it was purposefully named to discourage people, because nobody really wants to associate their baptism with a eunuch.

"The 'Cornelius' was the right choice. Named for the wealthy centurion of the Italian cohort that Peter baptized, this package cost quite a bit more, but after all, you are only baptized once (or more if you feel like it's necessary). The 'Cornelius' included the certificate with a frame upgrade, the candle with name in gold and a candle holder, plus a videotape of the baptism and an Egyptian cotton bath towel embroidered with the words "Remember your baptism" on it.

"You see what I mean?"

I did but I was a little distracted because as Pastor Nick talked, he kept looking over at me and not at the traffic, which was considerable. Also whenever he became excited about a point, he would push on the accelerator.

"You see what I mean?" he says, and the minivan lurches forward. "They don't even know what it is about. They forget the judgment."

"The judgment?" I say. "In baptism?"

"Yeah, read Luke. In the beginning of Luke, right before baptizing people, John says, 'I baptize you with water but he will baptize you with fire and the Holy Spirit.' Where is the fire in baptism? Everybody does the water but where is the fire?"

I tell him I have never really heard of the fire part of the baptism.

"Exactly," he says, punching the accelerator. "You see John's baptism—water baptism—is a baptism of repentance. It is the act of an individual. It is the starting point. But Jesus' baptism—fire baptism—is a baptism of judgment. It is the refiner's fire that burns away everything that is false, that has no life, that gives no life—burns away the shell and the lies, the vacuous detritus. John says this fire is unquenchable."

"That fire baptism doesn't seem like a very good thing." He looks at me like I have just said the dumbest thing in the world.

"What do you mean, not a good thing?"

I say, "You know, the judgment."

"The judgment is the very best thing. It comes with the mercy. Malachi says, 'For he is like a refiner's fire. He will sit as a refiner and purifier of silver and he will purify the descendants of Levi and refine them like gold and silver until they present offerings to the Lord that are righteous.' You see. It's all over the book—the mercy and the judgment. But you know what haunts me?"

At this point I'm not sure I want to know what haunts him. He doesn't wait for me to answer.

"12:49. 12:49 haunts me. I can't quite figure it out."

"Oh yeah, 12:49," I say, pretending I know what he is talking about.

"Luke 12:49," he says. "It is the only other place in Luke that talks about Jesus' baptism. I found it because I was looking up fire passages. It says, 'I came to bring fire to the earth and how I wish that it was already kindled! I have a baptism with which to be baptized and what stress I am under until it is completed.' It kind of sounds like Jesus is going to be the one baptized with fire, like he receives the judgment but that doesn't make sense."

We pull into his driveway. He turns off the engine, hits the garage door–opener button, and jumps out.

"Come on," he is practically running. I follow him. The garage door opens, slowly revealing a mess that must, I think, mirror his mind. More wood scraps and metal, more jugs of purified water, big water-cooler-type bottles, and more gas cans. The garage really smells like gas. There are all sorts of drawings tacked up on the wall and spread over the workbench, and the scripture verses he was quoting me are blown up to yard-sign size and tacked to the wall. He has circled and highlighted certain words ("fire" most frequently). On the wall I see spray-painted: "12:49?" In the middle of the garage is the mercy machine.

It is a wooden box the size of a phone booth or a coffin standing on end. There is a handle on the side like a slot machine but bigger and made of wood. The backside is removed, and I can see the inner workings—a mess of metal springs and copper pipes. There are two tanks fastened to the inner sides. One says "water"; the other says "gas." I moved around to the front. That's when I saw, mounted on the top of the mercy machine on a short pole, a metal crucifix about six inches tall. Coming out of the front is what looks like a showerhead. Big gold letters above it spell "mercy"; further down is a sort of metal nozzle sticking out. The word above it is "judgment."

Pastor Nick is watching me look everything over. He is grinning and bouncing up and down on the balls of his feet, his arms hugging himself. When I look at him, he starts in again with the frantic talking, moving around the mercy machine, showing me how it is supposed to work.

"You see," he says, "the Baptism Candidate stands in front like this and grabs the handle on the side and pumps it a bunch of times. This simultaneously builds up pressure in the tanks and winds up a spring. Then you step on this pedal and it releases the water, showering the person with water, really drenching them. Then the spring unwinds and the steel strikes this flint and lights the pilot and it goes around once more and opens the gas valve and it shoots fire out here.

"What do you think?" he says.

I say, "It, uh, seems like it would burn the Baptism Candidate."

He rubs his forehead, "Yeah," he says. "That's the part I can't figure out. I wish there was some way I could symbolically burn them, or have the fire just shoot out briefly, so it wouldn't burn them too bad. I thought about having the fire shoot out first, followed immediately by the water to put out the fire or cool off any burn, but I think theologically it wouldn't be correct. I think it will be ready to test next week."

He was quiet on the ride back to the coffee shop, but from the way his eyes were darting around and the occasional punching of the accelerator, I don't think it was quiet in his head.

I thought about calling him that next week, but I didn't have his phone number and realized I didn't even know his last name. The only time I had ever seen him outside the coffee shop was on that trip to his house.

On Thursday Pastor Nick walked into the coffee shop. I looked at him. He smiled his smile, but it was a bigger grin than I'd seen before. He had tested the mercy machine. He sat down at my table. From the looks of him, apparently what was untrue, shallow, and contained no life was his hair. The refiner's fire had also burned a good portion of his left arm. It was covered in a bandage up to his elbow. I also saw a bit of a gauze bandage sticking out of the collar of his shirt. "Tell me," I said.

"Well," he said, "I stood in position and I pumped the handle. I pumped it up pretty good until I could feel the pressure building up. Then I stepped on the pedal and nothing happened. I could hear the spring unwinding and then a little trickle of water came out. Then I heard a whoosh followed by the crackle of fire. It was burning inside the machine. I could see flames flickering out from under the bottom base and through all the seams on the sides. Then there was another whoosh, and fire was shooting out of the top, completely engulfing the crucifix. I should have run right then, but the crucifix started to turn a dull red; it was so hot that the crucifix went from red to orange to bright yellow before my eyes. It was amazing."

Pastor Nick continued: "I heard this loud crack and saw that the fire had burned through the front of the base, and the whole thing fell forward. I tried to jump back, but I wasn't fast enough. The showerhead came down on my arm and hand, and it was so hot that it burned me pretty good. The whole machine just collapsed on top of me. And the crucifix," he winced with pain, "the crucifix." He unbuttoned his shirt halfway and peeled off the big bandage on the left side of his chest to reveal a nearly perfect image of the Son of God branded deep in his skin.

"Man," I said.

"Yeah," he said. "I'm lucky to be alive. My clothes were on fire. I ran out of the garage and did the stop, drop, and roll on the lawn. The garage—totally gone. The house—completely gutted. Everything in it gone—everything."

"Man," I said again. "The mercy machine."

"Yeah," he said. "It worked perfectly."

Editor's Comment

The task of constructing a biography from scraps of paper and undated journal entries obviously leaves a lot of gaps and requires some speculation. This incomplete information has often been frustrating, but at times it has given me the freedom to imagine a life for Lamblove that it is becoming clear he did not live. I could picture him finally giving up after being taken away to the hospital at the end of "Separation." He had nothing. A more definitive end could not be imagined. I imagined him walking away—getting out of the hospital and getting in his car and just leaving town. Maybe taking Amy with him. Going somewhere else. Getting a job at a coffee shop and just saying, "The institution of the church is broken. The faith that created it is broken." At the end of "Mercy" he seems to not be walking away, but walking back. Returning. I will confess, I have come to feel some fondness for the Reverend, and I don't want him to go back. Lamblove, just walk away.

He doesn't listen to me. He seems to recast his revolution.

journal entry
(The Lord's Supper as
a Revolutionary Act)

A revolutionary act is unexpected. It is the radical surprise or the unexpected revelation of the obvious—something so ordinary and so taken for granted that when acted upon, it seems radical.

The sacrifice of Christ is such an act. This sacrifice, celebrated in the Lord's Supper, is at the same time so unbelievable and so expected. God gives God's own life for the ones God loves. What parent would not do this for her own child? It is the expected response, but to see it done, and on such a scale, and in such a definitive way, is revolutionary.

A revolutionary act includes people; it does not exclude them. The act of communion is often not communion at all but exclusion. But the banquet table in the Kingdom of God is open to all. It is peopled with those we don't know, understand, or like. Christ sacrificed himself once and for all, and when we remember that definitive act of love through the ritual of the Lord's Supper, there can be no qualifications in our invitation to the table. We should seek instead to find new words, new languages—a thousand new ways of inviting people to the table so that a thousand new people will feel welcome.

A revolutionary act trusts God to reveal God's self and trusts individuals to reveal themselves to God. The Lord's Supper generally takes place in the context of the community worship service. While this context is purposeful and meaningful, the individual's response to God is still an individual act. Participation should never be seen as a sign of who is in and who is out. The words and prayers before the ritual must never seek to convince or persuade the hearers to participate or not. The church is called to proclaim the Good News. The church is not responsible for clarifying, guaranteeing, or double-checking the Holy Spirit's revelation to individuals. Nor is it the church's right to demand some demonstration that the individual has received the Good News.

A revolutionary act is an invitation, not a threat. The revolution of mercy coerces no one, because the Good News is good, and therefore doesn't need to be forced on anyone. Before the communion ritual there can be no threats about the proper attitude of the heart or the sincerity of one's convictions. It is hard to gauge the sincerity of one's own convictions, to say nothing of another's. Christ says, "This is the blood of the new covenant I make with all of you." The heart of the gospel of Jesus Christ is about widening the circle, expanding the definition of "chosen," removing the barriers between 'them' and 'us.'

A revolutionary act is, finally, an act. An action. Not an idea, philosophy, notion, or intention, but an action. Ideas only change the world when acted upon. We are physical beings in a material world; acting something out makes it real. When we are asked to "do this in remembrance of me," we are asked to do something. The remembering does not take place simply in our minds.

This is a different kind of revolution. It is a quiet revolution.

sermon

The uncontrollable Love of God

MARK 16:1–8

And when the Sabbath was past, Mary Magdalene, and Mary the mother of James, and Salome brought spices, so that they might go and anoint him. And early on the first day of the week they went to the tomb when the sun had risen. And they were saying to one another, "Who will roll away the stone for us from the door of the tomb?" And looking up they saw that the stone was rolled back; for it was very large. And entering the tomb, they saw a young man sitting on the right side, dressed in a white robe; and were amazed. And he said to them, "Do not be amazed; you seek Jesus of Nazareth, who was crucified. He has risen, he is not here; see the place where they laid him. But go, tell his disciples and Peter that he is going before you to Galilee; there you will see him, as he told you." And they went out and fled from the tomb; for trembling and astonishment had come upon them; and they said nothing to anyone, for they were afraid.

. . . .

This is Easter. You are all loved. You are loved in an uncontrollable, inconceivable way. You are loved perfectly, by God who created you, through Jesus who has come to be with you, through God's Spirit who dwells among us.

God comes walking out of the desert alone so that we will not recognize God. Jesus does not look like God, and no one suspects until it is too late, when Jesus has once and for all destroyed the barriers between heaven and earth, collapsing the institutions and the rules that govern how God is supposed to act, destroying even the power of death to separate us from that love, removing forever the ability of institutions and people to control us, eliminating fear from death and fear from life. But to most of us, this love is a secret. Jesus sneaks around beside us, and loves us. When we act as if God has not changed the world, when we live in fear, with dread, goaded forward by an inner reserve of shame, Jesus is there, loving us secretly until we are ready to hear.

I have found out something about this secret love.

This love is present not only when I am overjoyed and filled with a profound sense of well-being, not only when I feel beautiful, super smart, and surrounded by people who think I am wonderful. This love is present when I am afraid of the world, when I am mean to people I care about or don't even know, when I look in the mirror and find that I am too fat, have a weird nose and crooked, coffee-stained teeth, when I feel like a loser, when I act like a loser.

Jesus is there, staying out of the way, loving me. Telling me always, whispering in my ear, "I love you. You are living in a lie—perfection and power do not exist. Imperfection and dependency is all there is. That is the place where everyone lives, and it is beautiful—it is freedom. Oh yeah, there is something else: I love you."

I have discovered that this love only remains a secret because I cannot hear what Jesus is saying. But Jesus does not get mad; Jesus does not talk louder; Jesus just keeps telling me secrets in my ear, "I love you. It is OK to be you. I love you." Jesus is not impatient, because Jesus believes one day I will hear. He believes that the love of God will not go unheard forever, that it will seep into my bones and fill the air around me until one day I will hear it. And when I hear something and turn around, I will see Jesus standing there, smiling.

This is Easter.

God does not come to be with us to intimidate us, overpower us, or impress us with great majesty. God does not come to earth to whip us into shape, to pump us up, to give us the competitive edge. God does not touch down in Jerusalem on a flaming chariot with the angels flying before a grand conveyance. God comes walking out of the desert at the beginning of this story alone, in the person of Jesus the Reconciler.

We know the trajectory of power and glory. We can track it; we know where it is going next. Sacrifice and humility is another story.

I want to be rich. I want to be famous. No. No. Of course that is the wrong thing to say. I am supposed to say I don't want to be rich. I just want to be comfortable. I want to provide a good life for my family. Have some security. Have just enough money to have the freedom to do whatever I want to do, which means about $1.6 million a year.

But honestly, when I am quiet and tell myself the truth, what I really want is to stare past the marvelous possibilities of my own wealth and personal power and to see out into the darkness to find a life where I am comfortable with what I have now and who I am now. Where I can find freedom in valuing people and relationships more than things. Where I want for others the same things I want for myself. Where I work for others to find the things that I want to find for myself. To find peace and freedom ultimately, not in the guarantee that I know the answers or how the story ends or the part I will play in it but in the knowledge that God has come to be with us and to love us in a way that we cannot control. I want to find meaning and passion in following the uncontrollable love of God, revealed in Jesus, wherever it takes me.

This is Easter. You are all loved. You are loved in an uncontrollable, inconceivable way. You are loved perfectly, by God who created you, through Jesus who has come to be with you, through God's Spirit who dwells within you.

This love is wily, uncontrollable, mysterious, willing, unshakable.

Post-Apocalyptic Praise Song, Part Three

Do you have to be awake for it to be a vision? What if you can't remember if you were awake or asleep when you saw things? What if when it was all over you woke up, but not like waking up from sleeping. This whole thing feels like waking up to me. The reason I am thinking about this is because the last vision or dream thing I had started with me waking up.

I woke up to the song. It was playing on my clock radio. I rolled over to look out the window to get my bearings. The sun stabbed at me. I rolled back over to look at the time. It was past two in the afternoon. That song on the radio? Then the announcer said something like, "This is post-rapture radio. We'll be here with you until we get it all figured out." Did it really happen? Did the world end? Was the meeting of the Commission Commission announcing that the world did not end premature? Was it the song they sang? Did it work? If so, why was I still here? Was I left behind? This might take some getting used to.

To be honest, being left behind wasn't that bad. It really wasn't that different. I thought there would be a lot less traffic and shorter lines at the grocery store, but it was about the same. Actually, I don't think I would have even noticed that the apocalypse had happened if it wasn't on the radio and in the paper. I was out pretty late the night before, and I slept most of the day so I guess I missed all the fire from the sky and rivers turning to blood and the mayhem resulting from all the people vanishing. They got it cleaned up pretty quickly.

There was a back-up on Selby Avenue, but I was walking so it didn't affect me. I did see a trash can on fire. Maybe that was from some brimstone landing in it. I was going to try and put it out, to do my part during this time of tribulation, to be a good citizen, but it looked kind of cool so I just left it.

At first when I read about the end of the world I tried to feel bad or sad or scared. I even put my newspaper down and yelled, "Nooo!" But my heart wasn't in it. I just felt kind of happy. It was weird but the world didn't feel as dark and scary as it had before. And then when I went outside to check it out, I realized I was practically skipping. It was exciting. A lot of other people were out too, looking around, and everyone was talking to each other, saying things like, "Man can you believe it? The end of the world. I never thought I would live to see it." And "Do you think we have to go to work?" It was like a snow day. It was nice because people aren't usually out on the sidewalk. Everyone is usually sealed up in their SUVs, honking at each other and giving each other the finger. But now people talk to each other. There's something to talk about, I guess.

It's kind of funny, because before the apocalypse if you said something to someone on the street, even like, "Do you know the time?" they would think you were weird or that you were trying to rob them or something. Most of the time they wouldn't even talk to you; they would just scowl at you, clutching their purse or feeling for their wallet, and walk away. Now you can go up to anyone, anywhere and say, "Too bad about the world coming to an end and the wrath of God being poured out on all nations" and it's perfectly normal. They will say, "Boy, you're not kidding."

There was a bit of a crisis at first because everyone was still getting used to living in the time of tribulation, and people weren't really sure what to do. There was a scare because people stopped buying stuff. There was confusion about whether or not you had to have the mark of the beast to go shopping, and no one knew where to get it.

The Commission Commission issued a press release that everyone should keep buying stuff for now and that C4! stores were having a post-rapture sale: "Everything must go!" There would be a press conference that night. All the leaders of Commission Commission were going to speak, to explain everything to everybody. I had read the book of Revelation quite a bit, but I wanted to bone up on what was going to happen (or what did already happen) so I could know what to look for.

I had Bibles at home and at the office, but I went a C4! bookstore to buy one. I didn't really want to go home to get one. It was pleasant being out and about and talking to people; it seems like one should be with other people in times of crisis. Plus I thought it would be fun to test the whole mark-of-the-beast thing.

All the C4! stores seemed pretty crowded. I guess the press release worked. In the bookstore they had a huge display of Bibles right in front, and they had a cash register set up next to it. They must have brought in extra help. There were a lot of people working to restock the Bible display. They were selling them almost as fast as they put them out. I could see more people working in back. They were ripping out all the pages of the Bibles except for the book of Revelation. I grabbed a copy and stood in line. When I got to the register, I held what was left of the Bible up to the cashier and said, "Hey, do I get a sixty-five percent discount on this?" She looked at me funny and not in a very friendly way. I said, "You know because there are sixty-six books in the Bible and there is only one left. It's a joke." She didn't smile. She took my money and said, "That's the only one you need from here on out."

It was about an hour before the press conference, so I went to this bar I like, where I knew I could watch it. It was crowded, too. The only place to sit was at the bar. I knew the bartender; his name was Chris. I sat down and said, "Chris, it looks like Armageddon makes people thirsty." He was too busy to pay attention. No one thinks I'm funny at the end of the world.

Chris gave me my usual, without his customary pseudo-detached, ironic comments, because it was so packed. That is when it hit me. What was Chris doing here in my dream—in my vision?

What was I doing in my neighborhood bar? In my neighborhood? I had awakened in my bed in my house. I had never been in my neighborhood in a vision before. I had never reflected on the visions while having a vision before. I had walked into that C4! bookstore like I had been there a hundred times, like it wasn't weird at all. My vision world had somehow leaked into my real world. I started to hyperventilate. I felt like I was having a panic attack.

"Breathe," someone said over my shoulder. I turned around and saw the smile. It was Idiot John. I looked at him with all the questions. "Just read what I wrote," he said, looking at the Bible on the bar.

It was still about forty minutes until the press conference, so I read. I had never found Revelation so interesting. It's like when you read a book that takes place in your city or see a movie where a scene was filmed on your block. But more than that, I noticed stuff that I never noticed before. The book is funny. It is sort of like a farce or a black comedy but with a really serious point.

I never got that the whole book is really about idol worship. That is what the whole book is about.

It starts off really grandiose. John says that God gave this message to Jesus, who gave it to an angel, and then the angel appeared to him and showed him this vision and told him to write it down as a message to these seven churches in a part of the Roman Empire that is basically Turkey.

So the message that God and Jesus and the angel want John to write to five out of these seven churches is: don't be such idol worshipers.

These churches were all in a pretty well-off part of the Roman Empire, and life in those cities was pretty good, pretty comfortable. So it was easy to give in to what was going on around them. The people in these churches had adopted the culture of Rome, and so the message of Revelation is that they are living by the values of the Empire and not the values of the Kingdom of God. They had Christianized the cults and culture of the Empire and could no longer see what they were doing.

The whole of the book is a telling and retelling of how the Roman Empire looks to one who has not been assimilated by it. It contains a constant call to repent and come out of Babylon. It says, you think the Empire is comfortable? You think wearing a toga with a fish logo on it is bearing witness? Wake up! Hear what the Savior has to say to the churches!

John writes that they have abandoned their first love; they eat the food sacrificed to idols. He says, "Wake up! You think you are rich and prosperous and you need nothing, but you do not see that you are poor and naked. Worship God, not the idol of power and money."

The book then goes on to paint this fantastic picture of all the horrible things that will happen to idol worshipers and all the great things that are to come for non-idol worshipers.

Here is the farcical part. The one who is going to mete out all this horror is introduced to John. The angel says, "See, look at the great Lion, the conquerer," and John looks and sees a lamb. A slaughtered lamb, no less. Not really as ferocious. In one line it says everyone hid in caves to escape the wrath of the lamb. The wrath of the lamb? What kind of wrath does a lamb have? Then this vision has all of humanity alternately worshiping idols and God. All of humanity worships the beast, and Satan, and the whore of Babylon. Then all of humanity worships God and the lamb. Back and forth, back and forth.

At the climax of the book, when all evil and the enemies of God are defeated by the lamb, the angel tells John that all the idol worshipers have been thrown into the lake of fire and that everyone will be invited to the marriage supper of the lamb. And you know what John's response is? He falls down and worships the angel. Idiot John! The angel says, "What are you doing? Get up.

Worship God, not me." Then there is another great battle with the beast, and all the idol worshipers are again slaughtered, and then God makes a new heaven and a new earth and comes and lives with all of his creation.

Yeah, the amazing, almost incomprehensible thing about the book occurs in chapter 21. After all these cycles of warning and judgment and calls to repent and come out of Babylon and live in the Kingdom of God, the opposite happens. The churches don't come out of Babylon, so God brings the Kingdom to them.

"Then I saw a new heaven and a new earth; for the first heaven and the first earth had passed away, and the sea was no more. And I saw the holy city, new Jerusalem, coming down out of heaven from God, prepared as a bride adorned for her husband; and I heard a great voice from the throne saying, 'Behold, the dwelling of God is with men. He will dwell with them and they shall be his people and God himself will be with them.' He will wipe away every tear from every eye there will be no more death or suffering or crying or pain" (Rev. 21:1–3).

In conclusion, Idiot John says the angel showed him all these beautiful things and said, "Blessed is the one who keeps to the words of the prophesy of this book." And you know what John's reaction is to this? He falls down and worships the angel again. I am not kidding. The conclusion to this book that calls all of humanity to wake up and come out of the Empire and stop worshiping the idols of the Empire so that they don't suffer eternal torture is that no one comes out of the Empire, so God brings the Kingdom of God to the Empire and promises to live with them and love them and wipe every tear from their eye.

And just in case you don't get the point, John finishes up by worshiping an idol. They were all trapped in the culture of the Empire and could not free themselves; they were all idol worshipers, even the great messenger of God. They couldn't help it.

This is it. This is the true story. Babylon and the New Jerusalem are not places; they are relationships. The Conspiracy does not want us to know this. They don't want people to see that Contemporary Culture is Babylon and that the church and Babylon are hopelessly enmeshed. They would be shocked at the suggestion that their values are in any way similar to the values of Contemporary Culture. In truth, the Babylonian relationship is what defines the Conspiracy. But it is not just the Conspiracy. We all live in the Babylonian relationship. We cannot free ourselves from the evil that we love. We cannot get ourselves to leave Babylon, so God comes to get us. The New Jerusalem comes down from heaven, and God dwells with us.

I heard the TV so I looked up. The press conference was starting. The same khaki pants—the same golf-shirted, sit-on-a-stool leader of the Commission Commission who spoke at the mega-mall-church and declared that the world did not end was now saying that they had made a miscalculation and there was some evidence that it actually did. He went on to say that in these terrible times, evildoers must repent and return to the churches so that they can be saved. That now is the time to put faith in the institutions that are best prepared to deal with this situation.

Someone asked a question: "What evidence, exactly, do you have that the world ended?" His eyes darted to the other khaki-pants-golf-shirts before he answered, "Well, actually, it is more of a hunch. It just seemed like the timing was right."

Another reporter followed up: "If the apocalypse has occurred and the rapture has taken place, how come you all are still here? How come you were left behind?" "Um," the Contemporary Christian khaki-guy cleared his throat. "Let me correct you. The sinners have been left behind. And the best we can figure is we've just been held back—it's different." I looked over at Idiot John. He was smiling. I asked him, "Is it really the end of the world?"

"It usually is," he said.

"John," I asked, "after all you saw in your vision, how could you still fall down and worship that angel?" He looked up at the TV and smiled, "I guess we just can't help it."

So this is what the end of the world is like. Like I said, being left behind isn't bad at all. It is really not that different from before the end of the world. Except I guess I'm happier.

journal entry
(I used to be so sure)

I used to be so steady. I used to be so sure. I used to know all the answers. I used to ride my bike with no hands; now I just concentrate on moving the pedals. I used to have belief as hard as a rock; now everything is soft and I only have a little faith. Only a little.

I used to be so rock-solid sure; I used to misunderstand so much. And I used to preach that misunderstanding, preach it hard like my rock of faith. I used to pound that misunderstanding hard until other people believed it.

I used to be so sure.

Now I preach questions and a little faith. And reaching out to take the steady hand of Jesus and reaching out to steady someone else. And forgiveness. I preach forgiveness. I do this not for any credit in heaven or for an eternal reward, but because this is how I try to live my life.

I try to have a little faith and two outstretched hands. A little faith and two outstretched hands.

~~Be sure~~

Editor's Comment

Listen Lamblove, you have every reason to be sure. You know what the Contemporary Christian Culture Conspiracy is up to. You know what they are capable of, and you know there is no way you are going to change it. It has been going on since the beginning. It is built on power, and you have no power. You will be left only with pain and a few people.

Editor's Comment
....

I took this first note from some scribbling on the back of what appears to be a partially burnt cowboy shirt. The second one was stuck to my shoe.

JOURNAL ENTRY
OR NOTE OR SOMETHING

Pain and a few people? I won't deny it, but there's so much more at stake. The pain is so small in comparison.

Final Undated Journal Entry
(These Are the People I Love)

It has been six months since I took my leave of absence. I have been working part-time at a coffee shop. The rest of my time was supposed to be dedicated to self-care and reorientation, but has been more occupied with red wine and Japanese cartoons.

And this. I have been writing in my journal, making notes on anything at hand, trying to document the truth about the Contemporary Christian Culture Conspiracy. But it has been miserable. You can't have a revolution in a notebook. I have to preach. You need people. But there are no people. No congregation. No relationships. I have written some sermons, but when you write a sermon for yourself, it ends up being a sermon about yourself, and that is not a sermon. You cannot put Christ in people's mouths if there are no people, and if there are no people, there are no mouths.

I have had some job offers. Well, one. A big mainline Protestant mausoleum church asked me to come and preach for them, and afterwards asked if I would be a candidate to replace their retiring eighty-year-old Senior Pastor. But the whole experience was death.

They didn't listen to my sermons any more than my Contemporary Christian Culture congregation did. Yes, I said *my*—they are my congregation. They are the people I love. You can't start a revolution with smart, bored people who are OK with everything and anything you do. You need smart, scared people for whom something matters, even if their hearts are filled with the Anti-Christ of the Conspiracy.

I have to get my job back. The Good News *is* good, and people *will* hear it. I believe it.

I'll just go back and tell them I have my compass pointing in the right direction, that I am back on the trail—or off the trail—blazing a new trail or finding an old one. Whatever—I'll say what I need to say. I feel so happy and in love with Jesus.

From an article published in
the <u>st. paul tribune</u>,
November 25, 2000

PREACHER DIES OF INJURIES

During an unexplained riot that broke out at the conclusion of the sermon yesterday morning at Middle Wood Evangelical Church, the Reverend Russell Rathbun sustained serious injuries. He was taken to the Middle Wood Urgent Care and later to St. Luke's Hospital where he was pronounced dead.

No one has been arrested in connection to the incident. Police questioned several congregation members but their names have not been released.

A visitor to the church's nine A.M. service reported, "The whole church, almost everyone in the church, seemed to get up at once and run toward the pulpit. It seemed like it had something to do with the sermon. I don't know, I have trouble paying attention to sermons, so I don't know."

A church custodian said the sanctuary of the church was damaged, "It looked like a bomb went off in there." No further information was available.

epilogue

I must have been dozing. I was not unconscious or anything like that. The injuries I sustained were not life-threatening. The doctor was initially worried about my lungs from the smoke inhalation, but he says they'll be fine. I have some pretty bad burns and a slight concussion. "Lucky," he said. They always say that.

When I woke up from the doze, she was standing at the foot of my hospital bed holding a thick white plastic bag to her chest, smiling sideways and shaking her head. It was hard not to smile back, and, realizing this, I shifted my eyes from hers to the plastic bag. She looked down too.

"Oh," she said, holding the bag out slightly in a half offering, half reverential gesture. "Clothes. Yours were, um, uh . . ."

"Burned?"

"Burned," she nodded a playfully emphatic yes. "Very burned."

"The hospital called. They said the church number was the only one they could find. They asked if you worked there, and they explained what happened. They said whoever picked you up should bring clothes. Pastor Bob said he thought you two were the same size."

Whether wanting to be helpful or merely complimenting himself, Pastor Bob was wrong.

Amy took care of the paperwork, and I followed her out to her car, shuffling in the hospital slippers, the short sleeves of the dusty-rose golf shirt down past my elbows, clutching the excess fabric at the waistband of the khaki pants in a wad to hold them up.

〉 〉 〉 〉 〉 〉 〉

What can I say, dear reader? One last conceit, hope, option: I believe in it—in the truth of it, even though it is unbelievable. It seems like someone had to die.

"Do you want the air conditioner on?" Amy asked, starting to roll up the car windows and then rolling them back down, illustrating the options. "Does it hurt much?" She reached toward my shoulder, stopping five inches away, patting the air, then making an "ouch" face. "The seat goes back if you want to lay down." Fussing she was. Making fussing gestures to comfort me. Wanting to do something. Amy.

She turned on the radio. "Can you hear that?" she asked, doing a little drumming thing with the flats of her fingers on the console between us, smiling at her hand, then at the rearview mirror, re-gripping the wheel at ten and two, exhaling with her shoulders, smiling straight ahead.

"Where should I take you?"

"Where are you going?" I asked her.

"I have to go back to the church," she said.

"Yeah, me too."

acknowledgments

This book would not have been possible without the encouragement and real work of many people. These are a lot of them. Dan Wilson, Brett Larson, Cyndy Rudolph, Jim Larson, Josh Wenck, Mark Stenberg, Chris Larson, Mike Rathbun, and Maria Di Meglio read early drafts (well, Maria is just learning how to read so I told most of it to her). Cheryl Johnson, all the family in Sorrento, Jackie Di Meglio, Pamela Wurtz, Matt Rathbun, Paul Pohelman, Doug France, Joel Green, Clark Morphew, Scott Brownlee, and Bob and Betty Rathbun contributed to my writing in various and significant ways past and present. Julianna Gustafson at Jossey-Bass helped transform the manuscript. Tony Jones gave it early life and made sure it kept breathing. John Soshnick, my attorney, confessor, and friend, did a lot of things I can't talk about. Debbie Blue always shows me the best ways to go and is willing to go there with me. And these are the others: the House of Mercy congregation, who are smart and kind and tolerant; the Louisville Institute for grant support; and, finally, Jeanne Di Meglio, who makes all the good things in my life possible.

The Author

Russell Rathbun is one of the preachers at House of Mercy Church. He lives in St. Paul, Minnesota, with his wife, two children, and their dog KoKo. He writes hymns and country-punk love songs, some of which have been published in the *Songs of Mercy* hymnal (Sister Black Press, 2003) and have been recorded by the House of Mercy Band. He is the host of a Grand Ole Opry–style Internet radio show that can be heard at http://misplacedmusic.org. His writing appears in the collection, *Life in Body* (Cathedral Hill Press, 2005).